THE AMAZING SIGHTS AND COLOURS OF ASIA

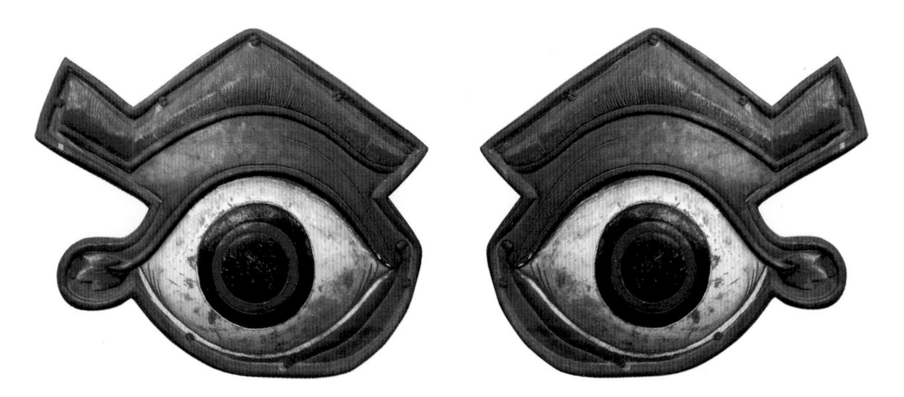

THE KATHMANDU VALLEY

THE AMAZING SIGHTS AND COLOURS OF ASIA

THE KATHMANDU VALLEY

GEOFF CLOKE

KERRY MORAN

LOCAL COLOUR

E-mail: ppro@netvigator.com

A CIP catalogue record for this is available from the British Library

Distributed in the United Kingdom and Europe by Hi Marketing, 38 Carver Road, London SE24 9LT. Fax: 020-7274-9160

Distributed in the United States by Seven Hills Book Distributors
Fax: (888) 777-7799

ISBN 962-8711-35-0

10 9 8 7 6 5 4 3 2 1

Captions: Geoff Cloke and Kerry Moran
Consulting editor: Kerry Moran
Editor: Georgina Shellum
Additional photography: Fredrik Arvidsson, p70 bottom, p95 bottom
Design: Geoff Cloke
Map: Tom Le Bas

Printed and bound in Hong Kong

(endpapers)
A devotee deep in prayer in the chilly morning mist at the Pashupatinath Temple on the banks of the Bagmati River, the holiest of all Hindi temples in Nepal. To be cremated here is said to bring the highest of good fortune and it is considered one of the four great Shiva shrines of the Indian subcontinent.

(title spread)
The magnificent gilt-copper roof of the Taleju Mandir in Durbar Square, one of the largest and finest temples in the Kathmandu Valley.

(opposite)
A young girl looking out from one of the intricately carved windows of the Degutalju Temple in Patan Durbar Square. The temple was built by Siddhu Narsingha in 1641.

(pages 6-7)
The all-seeing eyes of the Boudhanath Stupa survey all four directions from the outskirts of Chabahil, seven kilometres east of Kathmandu. With a diameter of over 100 metres, this is truly one of the great sights of the Kathmandu Valley and is a magnet for Nepal's Tibetan community, as well as pilgrims.

Their faith transforms it into a showcase of Buddhist practices — prayers wheels and beads, mantras and prostrations. All day long one can watch people walk clockwise about the stupa in ritual circumambulation. The monument is said to hold the relics of Kasyapa, a Buddha of a previous age.

(pages 8-9)
A large crowd watching the Gai Jatra festival standing on the stepped platform of five diminishing plinths which form the base for the Nyatapola Temple which, at 30 metres high, is the tallest temple in Nepal, and dominates Taumadhi Tol in Bhaktapur.

(pages 10-11)
Prayer wheels at the Swayambhunath, one of the most enigmatic of all the Valley's holy shrines which is situated to the northeast across the Vishnumati River. The area is reputed to be one of the oldest settlements in the Kathmandu Valley and is also one of the most important and sacred Buddhist shrines, the equivalent of the Hindu Pashupatinath.

(pages 12-13)
A typical farmer's cottage in a small hamlet just outside the village of Lubhu to the southwest of Kathmandu. The house is painted in the ubiquitous orange ochre paint, found throughout the Valley.

SUN
ENTRANCE

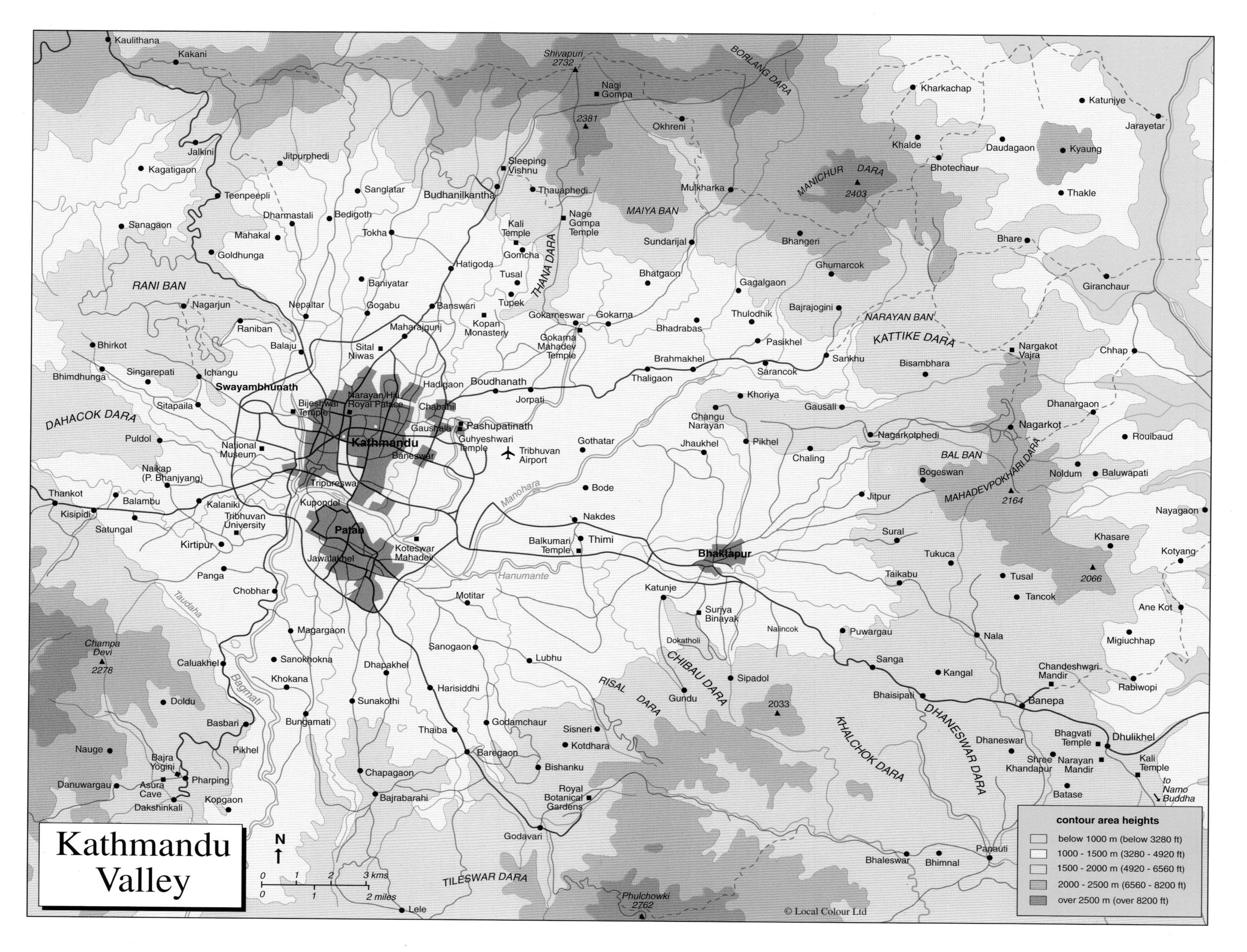
Kathmandu Valley
contour area heights
below 1000 m (below 3280 ft)
1000 - 1500 m (3280 - 4920 ft)
1500 - 2000 m (4920 - 6560 ft)
2000 - 2500 m (6560 - 8200 ft)
over 2500 m (over 8200 ft)
© Local Colour Ltd
N
0 1 2 3 kms
0 1 2 miles
Kathmandu
Patan
Bhaktapur
Swayambhunath
Boudhanath
Pashupatinath
Tribhuvan Airport
Kirtipur
Dhulikhel
Banepa
Nagarkot
Thimi
Budhanilkantha
Sleeping Vishnu
Changu Narayan
Godavari
Royal Botanical Gardens
Phulchowki 2762
Shivapuri 2732
Champa Devi 2278
Pharping
Dakshinkali
Chobhar
Bagmati
Manohara
Hanumante
Taudaha
Narayan Hiti Royal Palace
National Museum
Tribhuvan University
Kopan Monastery
Gokarna Mahadev Temple
Guhyeshwari Temple
Balkumari Temple
Koteswar Mahadev
Bijeshwar Temple
Sital Niwas
Nagi Gompa
Nage Gompa Temple
Kali Temple
BORLANG DARA
MANICHUR DARA
MAIYA BAN
THANA DARA
NARAYAN BAN
KATTIKE DARA
BAL BAN
MAHADEVPOKHARI DARA
DHANESWAR DARA
KHALCHOK DARA
CHIBAU DARA
RISAL DARA
TILESWAR DARA
RANI BAN
DAHACOK DARA
to Namo Buddha

Introduction

Life in the Kathmandu Valley provides so many things to gladden the heart: the flash of white on the northern horizon that signals the post-monsoon appearance of mountains unexpectedly, absurdly high . . . the devotion of a Buddhist monk prostrated full-length in front of the Boudhanath Stupa . . . the delight of children soaring up in great arcs on bamboo swings . . . the wild freshness the monsoon rains bring to the green rice fields . . . the piercing low tones of a conch shell blown by an itinerant ascetic wandering late at night . . . the golden light cast by butter lamps on serene faces intent on worship . . . the face of enormous beauty carved by some nameless, long-forgotten craftsman, discovered on a cobwebbed and shadowy temple strut.

Traditionally speaking, the Kathmandu Valley was Nepal, and to this day it is called Nepal by hill dwellers living as little as a day's walk away. It remains an outpost of civilisation, both traditional and modern, in the midst of a thoroughly rural country. Kathmandu is the capital of Nepal in every sense: political, economic, cultural, spiritual. The Valley is home to some 1.5 million people, a figure which increases yearly with the continuing arrival of virtually every Nepali with dreams of getting ahead.

The Valley's fertile bottomland is patterned with a patchwork of fields displaying the changing colours of the seasons. More and more farmland is being replaced by buildings, large and small, constructed of brick formed from the deep-red soil. The former kingdoms, now cities, of Kathmandu, Patan and Bhaktapur sprawl larger each year. Small farming villages dot the landscape as well, some inhabited by indigenous Newari people, others populated by Hindu caste groups or Tamangs. Ascending the sides of the surrounding hills are terraced fields, and a few remnants of the lush forests which only a few generations ago swept all the way down to the Valley floor.

Kathmandu's subtropical latitude combines with an altitude of 1,300 metres (4,300 feet) to generate tremendous biodiversity: 400 species of birds are found here, and over 1,000 species of plants. Leopards still roam the higher hills, as do deer and wild boar, and, rumour has it, a lone tiger on Shivapuri. Backing the entire vista are the soaring Himalayan peaks, the closest less than 50 kilometres (30 miles) distant. Protected by its great geographic barriers — the Himalayas to the north, the fever-ridden jungles of the Terai to the south — Kathmandu tantalised the West with its reputation as a hidden Shangri-La. Until a mountaineering reconnaissance expedition arrived in 1948, it remained the largest inhabited country unexplored by Europeans. The Valley was, however, long open to a diverse array of cultural influences. An entrepôt for trans-Himalayan trade, it linked the Indian culture of the Gangetic basin with that of Tibet, and by extension, China. Monks, traders, ambassadors, scholars, pilgrims and artisans all passed through here, leaving their mark.

Newari culture dates back an extraordinarily long period, to around the first century AD. Its Golden Age was the Malla Dynasty, which ruled the Valley for more than half a millennium — first as a unified entity; later as the three separate kingdoms of Kathmandu, Patan and Bhaktapur. Over the centuries the little city-states became increasingly cut off from reality, torn by constant bickering and political rivalries. In the late 18th century the Valley fell, as introverted societies are wont to do — straight into the lap of Prithvi Narayan Shah, the bold and tenacious ruler of nearby Gorkha.

People

Nepal's steep hills and deep valleys, and its extreme variations of altitude and climate have fostered, not only tremendous biodiversity, but great ethnic diversity as well. The national census lists 60 major groups, but there are many, many more tucked away in remote mountain valleys, each with their own language, traditions, customs and costumes. And inevitably, it seems, people from all these groups make their way to Kathmandu, where they converge at the trading crossroads of Asan Tol. A few hours spent observing faces here will convince you of Guiseppe Tucci's description of Nepal as "the ethnic turntable of Asia". Prithvi Narayan Shah waxed more poetic when he proclaimed, "My country is a garden for all types of people."

The Newars make up less than four percent of the national ethnic potpourri, but exert an inordinate amount of influence in their Valley homeland, where they constitute more than 40 percent of the population. The old quarters of the three towns remain predominately Newar, especially in Patan and Bhaktapur. Newars are easily distinguished by unique touches, like the

(top) *Statue of King Mahendra on the roundabout at the bottom of Durbar Marg.* (middle) *The Rani Pokhari, a large artificial pond built in 1670 to please a queen mourning the death of her son.* (bottom) *A painted stone chaitya, typical of these small monuments found all over the Valley. This one can be seen in Jamal neighbourhoods of Kathmandu.*

scarlet-bordered black skirts of Jyapu women, carefully draped to show off their blue-tattooed calves. Shrewd traders and superb farmers, the Newars are a highly successful group, but perhaps their greatest talent is artistic, expressed through metal, stone, wood, clay, and paint. Their fascinating culture is markedly different from that of the dominant Hindu caste groups. The Tibeto-Burman Newari language, with its own script and a rich classical literary tradition, bears little resemblance to any other tongue and comes in many different dialects — so many that a resident of Kathmandu has difficulty understanding a Bhaktapur dweller.

For the past two centuries, the Valley has been ruled by Hindu caste groups, Brahmins and Chhetris whose ancestors fled from Western India to Nepal following the Muslim invasions of the 13th and 14th centuries. Their language, Nepali, has become the lingua franca linking a polyglot country. Originally Brahmins were priests while Chhetris were warriors; today these traditional occupations are less likely to be followed, but the two groups together constitute Nepal's ruling class (both the ruling Shahs and the influential Ranas are of Chhetri stock).

Tamangs are another prominent feature of the urban landscape. These sturdy people are natives of the hilly regions surrounding the Kathmandu Valley, where they work as farmers and porters. In the city they may paint ritual Tibetan thangkas for the tourist trade, pedal brightly painted cycle rickshaws or drive the noisy little three-wheeled *tempos* which clog the streets. Traditionally they portered goods into the Valley, including motorcars for the Rana rulers, which were strapped to bamboo litters and lugged by teams of men over the hills from India. Buddhist by tradition, the Tamangs speak a Tibeto-Burman language and trace their ethnic roots back to Tibet.

The Valley's ethnic mix contains many more: almond-eyed Rai and Limbu from Eastern Nepal, whose Kiranti ancestors some historians believed ruled the Valley 2,000 years ago, stalwart Magars and Gurungs from the Central Hills; the famous Sherpas of Eastern Nepal, many of whom base lucrative trekking and tour businesses in Kathmandu; assorted Bhotia people from the northern mountains and the slender, dark-skinned peoples of the southern Terai.

The Urban Landscape

Centuries of Newari culture have created a cityscape that is a rich melange of cultural and religious influences. Tightly packed conglomerations of houses line the narrow brick-paved lanes of the old cities. Low doorways afford glimpses of peaceful courtyards centred around delicately carved stone *chaityas* or gilded family temples. Tiny shrines of red-daubed sacred stones or gilt-roofed temples appear every few steps, as do sunken water taps *(hiti)* and old open-sided resthouses *(pati)*. At the centre of each city are the Royal Palaces or Durbars, each facing a temple-strewn plaza or Durbar Square, which serves as a ceremonial centre and — more recently — a major tourist attraction.

The political fragmentation of the Three Kingdoms era had its problems, but it proved a boon for the development of art and architecture. Kings competed with one another to see who could raise the finest palace and the most lavish temples, seeking to glorify both themselves and their gods. The Malla rulers were public-spirited as well, sponsoring the construction of water tanks, taps, and resthouses, and providing endowments of land to fund their maintenance in perpetuity.

But the Newars' true genius lies in their skilful shaping of urban space. The real achievement is all around, in the intrinsic harmony and rhythm built up through centuries of organic growth. It is an aesthetic based on subtle curves and undulating waves, rather than straight lines and rigid angles. Rhythm is a palpable phenomenon, in the placement of buildings or the winding of streets. The subtle blending of materials adds its share — the harmony created by weathered brick, mellow stone and old wood, relieved by the occasional flash of a brass pinnacle or bronze temple guardian.

Against this serene backdrop are held the daily performances of life, enlivened by the seamless merging of public and private space. Streets and courtyards reveal people drying grain, spinning wool, bathing, enjoying an oil massage in the sun, scolding errant children, worshipping a deity, shouting imprecations at a cheating trader, nursing babies, hunting for lice (a favourite pastime), flirting, telling stories, smoking cigarettes, or shouting complicated instructions from a rooftop in full earshot of the entire neighbourhood.

Some scholars believe the stacked-roof temples found from China to Bali have its origins in the Kathmandu Valley. A seventh-century visitor marvelled at "multi-storeyed temples so tall one would take them for a crown of clouds." The modern Valley retains numerous examples of this basic graceful form, which is infused with elaborate symbolism not apparent to the naked eye. A temple's carefully measured ground plan is designed as a *yantra*, a mystic diagram of the cosmos; in this way, each embodies a bit of eternity in physical form.

(top) *An orange bas-relief of Dakani or the god of death.* (middle) *The front of a shop selling local metal craftwork in Patan Durbar Square.* (bottom) *A small Hindu shrine near Kamaladi.*

into delicately latticed screens and doorways lavished with rows of different motifs. Most dramatic are the slanted wooden struts which support the stacked roofs of temples. Carved into the form of the resident deity, they serve as a sort of divine billboard advertising the presence of a particular sacred manifestation. The largest corner struts sport winged griffons with horned heads and erect phalli.

Due to the Valley's pervasive syncretism, temples may be Hindu or Buddhist, or quite commonly worshipped by followers of both. Take the prettily decorated little gilt-roofed shrine adjoining Swayambhunath Stupa, one of the busiest in the Valley. Buddhists revere its resident deity as Harati; Hindus know her as Sitala. For both, she is the fearsome goddess of smallpox, a dread disease which swept the Valley well into this century. The recent eradication of smallpox has not deterred the steady stream of devotees who continue to supplicate the goddess with offerings of duck eggs, grain and yoghurt.

A uniquely Buddhist monument is the hemispherical stupa or the smaller, more elaborately carved stone chaitya. Both stupas and chaitya have their origins in the ancient Indian burial tumuli, but the eyes painted along the square base of stupa spires are a uniquely Nepali touch. Generally these eyes manage to convey the desired impression of wisdom and compassion, but there are also squinting stupas, sleepy stupas, farsighted stupas — even (in the case of Chabahil) a stupa with a light bulb dangling down over its third eye.

A final aspect: temples are not sacrosanct shrines to be entered only on Holy Days, but are interwoven into the fabric of urban life. Fruit and vegetable sellers spread their wares on the lower steps of Durbar Square's temples, while children fly kites from the higher levels and cavort across the stone guardians. The more active shrines, like that of the powerful goddess Nara Devi, are visited by a stream of worshippers throughout the day: women bearing their daily offerings, men touching their caps in a brief gesture of respect, supplicants seeking special favours.

Religion

The majority of Nepalis are Hindu (the country proudly calls itself "the world's only Hindu kingdom"), but religious syncretism and a generally mellower take on life gentles the orthodox Hinduism of neighbouring India into a rich and fascinating blend influenced by Buddhism and ancient animistic beliefs. Day in the Valley's old towns begins with the clanging of temple bells and the sight of women scurrying between neighbourhood temples with brass trays of flower petals, red *tika* powder and uncooked rice, which provide the basis of worship for peaceful deities. Other divinities, like the terrifying Bhairab, a form of Shiva, and the fearsome goddess Durga, demand more significant gifts. At the forest temple of Dakshinkali on the southern fringes of the Valley, Tuesdays and Saturdays are orgies of blood sacrifice. Worship, or *puja*, is carried out to propitiate the gods. To ignore them brings the risk of illness, misfortune and possibly death; to cultivate their favour can bring happiness and prosperity.

The gods are found everywhere in the Valley, not just in temples but in rivers, rocks and stones, in the hearth of homes and even buried in the household trash dump. Like humans, they have their own characters, playful or sly, fearsome or gentle. Ultimately all are considered expressions of the supreme and formless reality called Brahman. Deities manifest in larger-than-life forms, their multiple limbs and heads symbolising their complex powers. Each is easily identified by his or her own attributes, implements, emblems and animal vehicles. The mainstays of the Hindu pantheon include Shiva the Transformer, who embodies the powerful energies of birth and death; Vishnu the Preserver, a gentler manifestation who appears in ten main forms, and the sly trickster Ganesh, the elephant-headed Lord of Luck.

Beneficent goddesses are propitiated as well: the lovely lotus-eyed Lakshmi for wealth, or Brahma's consort Saraswati for the knowledge obtained from study. But the Nepali imagination seems to be most captivated by the fiercer manifestations of feminine energy —black-faced Kali, who squats atop a corpse with her tongue lolling, or the regal and courageous Durga, whose slaying of the buffalo-demon is celebrated in the great annual festival of Dasain each autumn.

Hinduism and Buddhism exist side by side in the Valley, and have done so peaceably for centuries. Seventh-century Chinese visitors marvelled at the way "Buddhist convents and the temples of Hindu gods touch each other". In the modern Valley there is hardly an orthodox temple to be found — shrines serve visitors from both religions and diverse cults, while Buddhist chaitya and Shaivite stand side by side in courtyards. Buddhism manifests in two forms in the Valley, both of them belonging to the highly complex Vajrayana school based on ancient tantric practices.

Tibetan Buddhism is the other form, an iconographically rich and complex series of practices involving deities, both fierce and gentle, who embody the entire range of human capacities. The Valley's Tibetan Buddhist population swelled following the Chinese invasion

(top) *The whitewashed walls surrounding the shikara-style Narayan Temple built in 1793, make its shady courtyard a peaceful, park-like haven.* (middle) *A street in old Kathmandu leading to Indra Chowk.* (bottom) *Jana Bahal, a classic Newar temple that honours Seto Machhendranath, a form of the compassionate bodhisattva Padmapani Lokeswara. Jana Bahal's charm lies in its fantastic metalwork.*

capacities. The Valley's Tibetan Buddhist population swelled following the Chinese invasion of Tibet in the late 1950s, when thousands fled across the Himalayas to take refuge in Nepal. Major Tibetan communities are now centred around the Buddhist stupas of Boudhanath and Swayambhunath, as well as the old refugee camp of Jawalakhel, south of Patan. It was Tibetan skills that started Nepal's important export industry of hand-knotted woollen carpets. Over the years, traditional Tibetan patterns and hues have been adapted to Western tastes, and nowadays the looms are usually worked by Nepali women.

Apart from, or rather, in addition to, the many Hindu and Buddhist deities, Nepalis live in a world of invisible forces: the *naga* or serpent deity which guards underground wealth; *deutaa* or local spirits which can bring good fortune or suffering, and the Newari Mai and Ajima, ancient "mother" and "grandmother" goddesses who must be propitiated with blood sacrifice. And practically every community has its suspected *boksi* or witch, who may be male or female, and who serves as a convenient scapegoat for misfortune and illness. To deal with this often malevolent universe, people rely on *jhankris* or shamans, who mediate between them and the many invisible forces. Jhankri-ism is so pervasive it's been called "Nepal's third religion".

Festivals

With so many gods, it is only natural that "every other building is a temple, every other day a festival," as an 18th-century English visitor to Kathmandu observed. The annual cycle of festivals shapes the year, bringing colour and magic to daily routine. Festivals invariably involve puja, offerings of flowers, rice and red tika powder lavished on the particular deity of the day. Great feasts of curried and fried food accompanied by mountains of rice are dished out onto disposable plates fashioned of stitched leaves (100 percent organic and biodegradable). Special bathing festivals allow crowds of shivering devotees to purify themselves in sacred rivers; or sometimes it is the holy image of a deity which is laved with mixtures of symbolic liquids. *Yatra* or processions march through the streets, accompanied by the drums, flutes and cymbals of Newar musicians, or by palanquins bearing images of deities.

The yearly festival cycle has its highlights: the oil lamps flickering on Patan's Krishna Mandir for Krishna Jayanti; the gay masquerades of Gai Jatra; Teej's gorgeous display of singing, dancing, clapping women in brilliantly coloured saris; the Hindu ascetics of various bizarre descriptions who descend upon Pashupatinath for Shiva Ratri and the cheerful crowds that ring Boudhanath Stupa at Tibetan New Year. For Valley residents, the greatest of all festivals is Indra Jatra, a week-long celebration held in old Kathmandu on the full moon following the monsoon's end. The air has turned fresh and clear, and the moon pours its silver light onto streets stalked by troupes of masked and costumed dancers. Old images of the god Bhairab are put out on display, temples are illuminated, wild crowds tug the Kumari's great wooden-wheeled chariot, and magic is most definitely in the air.

Locations

A pity that some visitors never see this aspect of Kathmandu. For many, Kathmandu is synonymous with Thamel, the busy tourist district north of the old town where one can buy every conceivable type of hat, map, turquoise bracelet, or embroidered T-shirt, to name only a few specialities. Thamel incarnates the opposite of the maxim "Do a few things, but do them well." On the contrary, you can get virtually everything here, but little is well done, and even less is really Nepali.

Just a kilometre or so south is another world entirely — old Kathmandu, a warren of interlinked lanes and courtyards and bazaars selling items both necessary and delightful. An endless stream of pedestrians sweeps through these, shopping for saris or soap or nails or any of the hundreds of other objects glimpsed through the wooden doorways. The ground floor of city dwellings serve as shops, or sometimes as workshops for artisans, bronze workers or silversmiths who skilfully anchor the piece they are working on with their toes.

It is absolutely essential to spend a morning, afternoon or evening wandering the old city, exploring its little markets specialising in little things. The Bead Bazaar, for example, tucked behind Indra Chowk, where Muslim traders preside over shimmering strands of glass beads and village women spend hours picking out the perfect necklace. Down the road in Makhan Tol are the cloth vendors, each displaying a rainbow assortment of fabrics. Round another corner at Bedhasingh is the "pottery temple," its lower steps covered with an assortment of pots, urns, jugs, jars, and containers of unglazed terracotta. Across the way is a string of shops selling *kapas*, the fluffy cotton used to stuff pillows and mattresses.

Kel Tol, the short stretch of road between Asan and Indra Chowk, is particularly fascinating. Part of the old, old trade route linking India and Tibet, the street is a riot of colour — draped

(top) *A street in Thamel, the main tourist area in Kathmandu.* (middle) *A pair of temple lions guarding the entrance to Kwa Bahal, or Golden Temple, one of the most spectacular of the many Buddhist monasteries to be found in and around Patan.* (bottom) *A guard stands near to the Taleju Mandir Temple in Kathmandu's Durbar Square.*

saris and shawls, rows of brilliant bangles, peacock-feather fans, tinsel decorations for celebrations and festivals, great sacks of turmeric and their yellow-dusted sellers, bundles of rope incense and huge brown cannonballs of soap, sticky brown heaps of *gur*, stacks of plates fashioned of green leaves stitched with bamboo fibres, garlands of marigolds and the orange-tinted heads of very recently slaughtered goats.

The nexus of all this activity is the trading centre of Asan Tol. Its vegetable sellers were evicted several years ago to make more room for traffic in a horrendous municipal decision, but crowds still swirl around the little Annapurna Temple, a gem of elaborately wrought metalwork dedicated to the goddess of the harvest. Old Kathmandu is breathtaking, especially early in the morning, when invisible temple bells clang from the winter mist, or on a summer evening when everyone's out on the street.

Across the Bagmati River, the former kingdom of Patan is linked to Kathmandu by suburban sprawl, but it retains its old-fashioned, otherworldly air. Historically known as the "City of Artists," it houses an active community of craftsmen who continue the tradition of skilled metalwork — everything from brass water jugs to fine bronzes crafted using the lost-wax process. Patan's huddled buildings, linked by the mellow tones of weathered brick, wood and tile, share the harmonious patina lent by age. The city's spacious courtyards house scenes that could be from medieval times.

The city remains a stronghold of Buddhist Newars, as demonstrated by the stupas, chaityas and shrines which dot the urban landscape together with old bahal, former Buddhist monasteries now occupied by communities of married "monks" who live with their families in the quadrangular quarters built around a central temple. The gilt-plated façade of Kwa Bahal, popularly known as the "Golden Temple," is an extravaganza of the finest Newari metalwork. An even more important, though less lavish, site is the stately shrine of Raato Machhendranath, Patan's most beloved deity. The strange red image of the god resides here for only six months of the year. The other six months it is ensconced in Bungamati, a thoroughly Newar village some six kilometres south of Patan.

Patan's Durbar Square has been acclaimed the finest of all the Valley's royal plazas by generations of visitors. It is indeed an astonishing assemblage of temples constructed of stone, wood and brick, lightened by the bright flash of rooftop pinnacles. Among the most marvellous structures is the naga-rimmed royal bath of Tulsi Hiti in the palace courtyard of Sundari Chowk. Sinuous stone snakes writhe along the top of curved walls inset with niches upon which stand superb small sculptures of deities in stone and metal, over five dozen in all. The exquisitely detailed 17th-century palace compound consists of a series of linked courtyards adorned with woodcarvings of the highest order.

Bhaktapur, on the other hand, embodies concentrated countryside. Fourteen kilometres east of Kathmandu, it remains surrounded by fertile fields that have long been considered the best farmland in the Valley. The third of the triumvirate of ancient kingdoms, Bhaktapur remains the most authentically in touch with its rural heritage. Some 90 percent of its population is Newari — Hindu Newars this time — and over half belongs to the Jyapu subcaste of peasant farmers. This ethnic cohesiveness has done much to preserve a rich cultural life rooted in ancient traditions.

Bhaktapur's tall red-brick houses are festooned with necklaces of drying corn, firecracker-red strings of chilli peppers, and chains of fermented dried greens called *gundruk*. Few vehicles ply the city's red-brick streets, which are filled with people doing all sorts of interesting things — drying grain, making pottery, dyeing skeins of wool. It's difficult to believe that this is an urban environment with one of the highest population densities on Earth. The tight concentration of people into a limited space conserves precious farmland, and is a characteristic of Newari cities. In the case of Bhaktapur, it seems to have had exceptional cultural results.

Bhaktapur's Durbar Square, while palatial in size, seems oddly empty. The devastating 1934 earthquake which shook the Valley left much of this city in ruins and wiped out fully half of the square's ornate monuments. The neighbouring plaza of Taumadhi Tol is much more integrated into the urban fabric. Here is the towering five-storeyed temple of Nyatapola, the tallest in Nepal, and another handsomely proportioned shrine to Bhairab.

Around the corner in the open-air atelier of Bolachha Tol, pottery of all shapes and sizes, in every stage of being formed, is being finished or refined. Muscular men knead unyielding lumps of black clay into submission, while skilled potters slap a handful of earth on their whirling wheels and miraculously cause it to bloom into a vessel.

As a stroll through the surrounding countryside soon reveals, life in the Valley follows a rhythm dictated by the seasons and the different kinds of fieldwork that accompany each. The advent of the summer monsoon brings long lines of workers into the flooded rice fields to

(top) *A vendor selling "singing bowls" in Basantapur.* (middle) *A decorative flower pot in a restaurant in Patan Durbar Square.* (bottom) *Crowds watching the Gai Jatra festival in Bhaktapur.*

plant the green shoots in the warm mud. A month later the vibrantly coloured fields are set amid the floating mirrors of flooded terraces. The clear, sunlit skies of autumn arch over a golden harvest season, when everyone joins together to bring the ripened grain in on time. The coldest months see fallow fields of stubble grazed by livestock herded by shouting children, but nothing stays unplanted in the fertile Valley for long.

Any visit to the countryside, however brief, also reveals that women are the workers of Nepal. They do their share of planting and harvesting as well as most of the weeding and maintenance of crops, carry water, wood, and huge mountains of fodder to feed their livestock, bear the children and care for them, do the laundry (by hand), cook the meals (over a wood fire), and process the food they have grown. The men pitch in at the peak work seasons of planting and harvest, but otherwise the main responsibility for the smooth running of life seems to fall on women's shoulders.

Holy Places

The Valley's singular mix of religions is best sampled in situ, at three of its greatest shrines. Each is dedicated to a different religion, and each displays a distinctly different character. The great stupa of Boudhanath in the eastern Valley is a superb site from which to observe the exceptional devoutness of Tibetan Buddhists, who can be seen performing the many sacred ceremonies their culture has refined.The crowd that endlessly circles the stupa moves clockwise, keeping the monument on its right as a sign of respect. This performance of *kora* or ritual circumambulation is a therapeutic combination of mild exercise, social stimulation and religious merit. Participants may finger prayer beads or spin the embossed copper prayer wheels, chat with a friend or even take their lhasa apso out for an airing as they stroll in circles. On full-moon nights the number of worshippers increases, and little stands are set up with butter lamps one can light for a few rupees to generate more merit.

Perhaps because it lies along the old Kathmandu–Lhasa trade route, Tibetans have always gravitated to Boudha. At least a half-dozen new monasteries are visible from the topmost level of the stupa, their ritual halls *(lhakhang)* hosting frequent prayer ceremonies of chanting monks accompanied by sonorous horns and thudding drums. Further in the distance is Kopan Monastery, where Western students gather each fall for a month-long meditation seminar. With its wide variety of teachers and practices, Boudha is the premiere site for the study of Tibetan Buddhism.

The western side of the Valley is guarded by the ancient hilltop shrine of Swayambhunath, said to have been built over the site where the legendary lotus blossom first emerged from that long-ago lake. Certainly Swayambhu is among the most ancient sites in the Valley, its historical roots lost in the mists of time. It's a steep, hard climb up the 365 worn stone steps to the very top of the hill. The stupa platform is enriched by centuries of royal gifts, including a giant gilded vajra and Buddha images constructed of carved and fitted stone blocks. Royal wealth was also lavished on the five little gilded shrines attached to the stupa's dome, one for each of the Pancha Buddhas who are associated with the five elements. Swayambhu is at its finest on a spring evening.

At the Hindu temple of Pashupatinath on the banks of the Bagmati River, Shiva is ruler. Pashupatinath, "Lord of the Beasts", is one of his many guises, the focus of an ancient Indian cult which today serves as the official patron of Nepal. Three millennia of Hinduism are concentrated here, in temples and little stone shivalayas housing carved linga, the quintessential symbol of Shiva. At once the destroyer and transformer of Hinduism, Shiva embodies all the powerful, dark and regenerative forces of nature. The deeply interwoven associations between his most holy shrine and death seem only appropriate. To die on the Bagmati's bank at Pashupatinath is said to bring the highest good fortune — release from the cycle of birth and death. The terminally ill are often carried down to pass their last moments with their feet in the water.

The Bagmati is considered Nepal's spiritual equivalent of India's sacred Ganges. Despite the horrific pollution created by raw sewage and industrial wastes, crowds of devout Hindus still gather here for ritual bathing, particularly for the festival of Shiva Ratri each February. The same period sees the arrival of crowds of sadhus, Hindu ascetics who may be holy men or slightly crazed eccentrics — often a combination of both. Some are clad in orange robes; others in a loincloth or nothing at all, smearing their bodies with ashes gathered from cremation pyres. They may perform peculiar penances, standing up for years on end or subsisting on a diet of only milk.

Its superb cultural wealth has led the Valley to be often called an "open-air museum." Its 570 square kilometres (220 square miles) are littered with temples and shrines and ancient stone sculptures that anywhere else would be safely encased behind glass, but here they are

(top) *A girl making an offering to a small Ganesh image which is covered with many layers of dark red* sindhur *or tika powder.* (middle) *Even shops selling beer have brightly painted doors.* (bottom) *A locked door guarded above by a brightly painted image of the classical* kirtimukha *or "Face of Glory".*

still actively worshipped, or simply taken for granted. In fact, the Valley is far better than a stuffy museum — it's a vibrant traditional culture that has somehow managed to survive into the new millennium.

The Modern Valley

What the next millennium will bring is less certain. Observers glumly predict the imminent demise of ancient traditions due to the pressures of modernisation. Such sentiments ignore large chunks of the inconvenient truth, such as the fact that a brown, smoky haze obscured Himalayan views during those supposedly halcyon 60s days, because most Kathmandu residents at the time cooked on wood fires. Yes, there is air pollution nowadays; and no, it is not the worst in Asia, no matter what some residents might claim. Caught up in the vortex of the admittedly ugly modern Asian city that is New Kathmandu, it's easy to forgot the Valley that lies beyond the smoke-belching of Putali Sadak — the harvest scenes straight from a Breughel painting, the rice-planting songs, the ancient deities and the blood sacrifices and the long low growl of monastery horns.

The modern world has definitely come to the Valley, and still a certain cultural strength and resilience endures, living on in traditions like the worship of the Kumari, a living virgin goddess. A dozen villages and towns in the Valley follow this ancient custom, but the most sacred of all is the Raj Kumari of Kathmandu, a little Newari girl chosen for her uncanny self-possession and flawless appearance as described in an ancient text: "Thighs like a deer, chest like a lion, neck like a conch shell, eyelashes like a cow, and body like a banyan." Once the high priests have determined her to be a suitable vehicle for the goddess — she may be as young as two years old — she is initiated and enshrined in the 18th-century Kumari Bahal adjoining the old Royal Palace.

Though she is of the Sakya caste of Newars and therefore Buddhist, her devotees believe her to be the Kumari incarnate Taleju Bhavani, a powerful form of the Hindu goddess Durga. Devotees come daily to worship her, women hoping for the boon of fertility or their children's health, and men seeking worldly power. The little Kumari reigns until the shedding of blood, through loss of a tooth or more commonly menarche, signals the goddess has left her body. Another young girl is chosen, and the former Kumari is free to lead an ordinary life.

Kathmandu is in some ways like this newly liberated Kumari — come of age and released from its traditional roles, freed into a less-romantic life which offers greater, if more uncertain, opportunities.

Many forces encroach upon the Valley's traditional culture. Most apparent are the obvious modernisations brought by the internal combustion engine, television and tourism. Less visible, perhaps, but more pervasive is the "Sanskritisation" created by social pressures from other Nepali ethnic groups, particularly the dominant hierarchy of the Brahman and Chhetri ruling castes. But somehow, the city retains its charm. A traffic snarl untangles to reveal its source, a caparisoned elephant bearing a regal red-and-gold-clad bride, and any impatience evaporates in a burst of pure pleasure. Another traffic jam is caused by a gaily dressed wedding band marching at a leisurely pace down the street, its trumpeters blaring out a tuneless melody punctuated by the ear-splitting thump of a bass drum. Or sometimes it's just the resident elephant of the Jawalakhel Zoo, slowly plodding home in the left-hand lane with its daily fodder. Sacred cows do their part to snarl city traffic, and snake charmers and itinerant sadhus play the crowds, while painted beggars lay on the sidewalks waving their stumps in search of baksheesh.

Contrast is the only thing one can take for granted in Kathmandu. Helmeted riders manoeuvre their motorcycles around the ancient shrine of Ashok Binayak, performing the traditional good-luck circumambulation made before departing on a journey. Cable dishes sprout from tiled roofs, and giant neon signs block views of old domed temples. What can one say about a place that produces at least seven major soft drinks and six types of beer, but can't come up with potable tap water? Or where an annual public holiday shuts everything down once a year so that gangs of young men can roam the streets, tossing buckets of water on passers-by and smearing them with red powder? What kind of comment can one make about a place where the Natural History Museum exhibits stuffed rats, where a revolution (the 1951 one) replaced an oligarchy with a monarchy, and where a Communist government periodically rules over the "world's only Hindu kingdom." How to understand a place that supports the Kumari and cable television with equal aplomb?

Faced with all this, one is forced to resort to Nepal's unofficial national slogan: "*Yo Nepal ho,*" "This is Nepal," accompanied by a slight heave of the shoulders that shrugs off its quirkiness as a matter of course. Truly the Kathmandu Valley is Nepal, complete in all its grime and glory.

(top) *A typical* sattal, *or village public resthouse and meeting place in Sankhu. At the end of the monsoon season the roofs of these guesthouses are often covered in a mass of vegetation.* (middle) *A beautiful stone Ganesh carving.* (bottom) *Mothers waiting to enroll their children in school near Indra Chowk.*

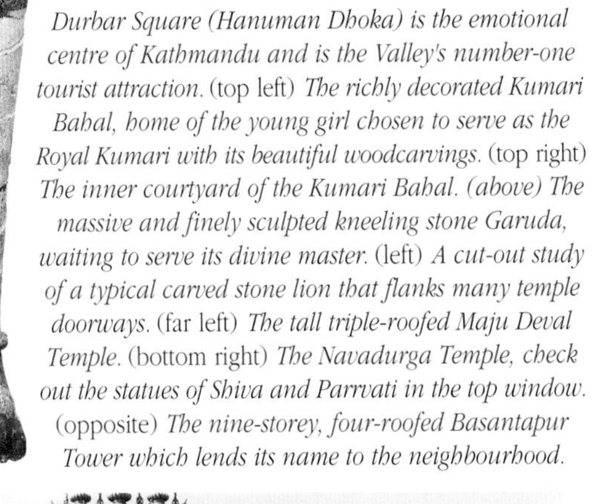

Durbar Square (Hanuman Dhoka) is the emotional centre of Kathmandu and is the Valley's number-one tourist attraction. (top left) *The richly decorated Kumari Bahal, home of the young girl chosen to serve as the Royal Kumari with its beautiful woodcarvings.* (top right) *The inner courtyard of the Kumari Bahal.* (above) *The massive and finely sculpted kneeling stone Garuda, waiting to serve its divine master.* (left) *A cut-out study of a typical carved stone lion that flanks many temple doorways.* (far left) *The tall triple-roofed Maju Deval Temple.* (bottom right) *The Navadurga Temple, check out the statues of Shiva and Parrvati in the top window.* (opposite) *The nine-storey, four-roofed Basantapur Tower which lends its name to the neighbourhood.*

बसन्तपुर
BASANTAPUR

While exploring the main Durbar Square take time to study the beautiful and intricate carving which Nepal is famous for, in particular the Shiva-Parvati Temple and the wing of the old royal palace, crowned with a small pagoda and housing a row of thangka *shops on the ground floor. The second-storey windows are classical masterpieces. Glance at the last set of windows on the corner, where kings once sat and watched their subjects. The inset carved ivory and gilded metal were hidden under layers of dirt until the palace was restored in 1975.*

LOVELY THANKA
MONASTERY
MANDALA
THANKA SHOP

(above) *Rhesus monkeys roam most temple grounds where they climb all over the buildings and also beg for, or steal food.* (top right) *A soldier guards the entrance to the Hanuman Dhoka.* (right) *Hanuman, the Monkey King of the Hindu epic* Ramayana *lends his name to the main entrance to the royal palace. Robed in red and shaded by a royal umbrella it is difficult to recognize the features of a monkey beneath an ever-thickening layer of* sindhur *powder.* (left) *Looking inside the walls of the Telegu Mandir Temple.* (below) *A bronze lion or griffon guardian.* (bottom left) *A typical stone carving of a temple lion.* (bottom) *The embossed golden gates to the Talegu Mandir.*

It is well worthwhile exploring the little-known area in South Kathmandu along the banks of the Bagmati River running from Patan Bridge to the big old Kaalo Pul footbridge (top left). (top middle) *A red-faced Monkey King guards the entrance to a Ramchandra Temple.* (top right) *Mahadev Mandir Temple.* (bottom left and right) *Everyday life at Tindeval by the Hanuman Ghat.*

(opposite) *The garishly painted Kaalo Bhairab in Durbar Square, a huge bas-relief adorned with six arms and a garland of human heads.*

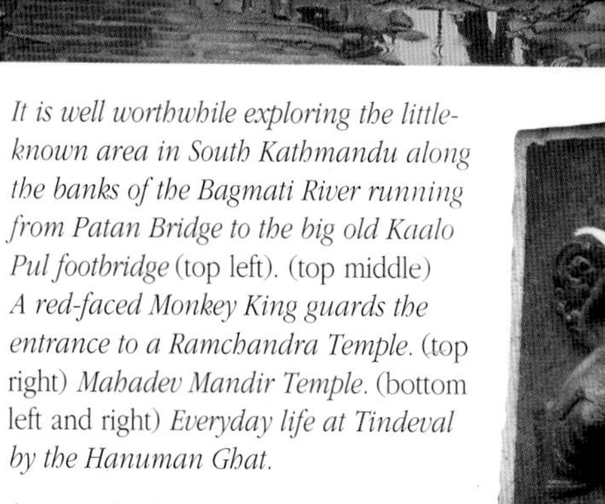

The golden spire of the Swayambhunath Stupa popularly known as the "Monkey Temple", crowns a wooded hillock that has been a holy site since at least the fifth century. The 365 worn stone steps that lead to the summit are guarded by pairs of animals — garudas, *lions, horses, elephants and peacocks.* (below) *an intricately carved and gilded tympanum or* torana *seen over entrances to temples or palaces throughout Nepal. The entrance to Swayambhunath is dominated by a great gilt vajra with a stone base which is ringed by carvings of the 12 animals that make up the Tibetan cycle of years.*

(left) Delicate carved wooden latticework above a an open resthouse where families prepare offerings to the goddess of smallpox, Sitala. The courtyard of the Swayambhunath is a veritable museum of sculptures and delicate woodcarving.

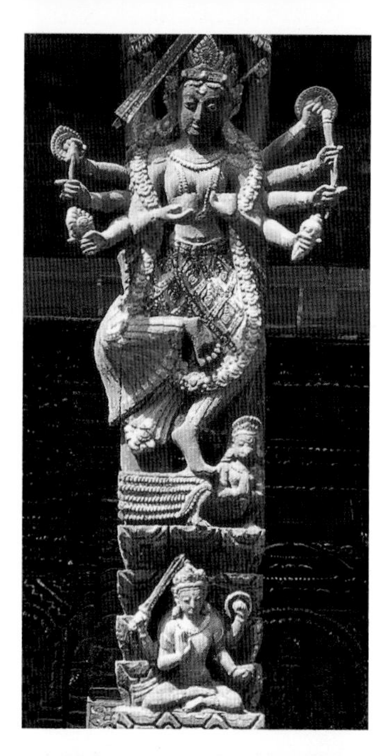

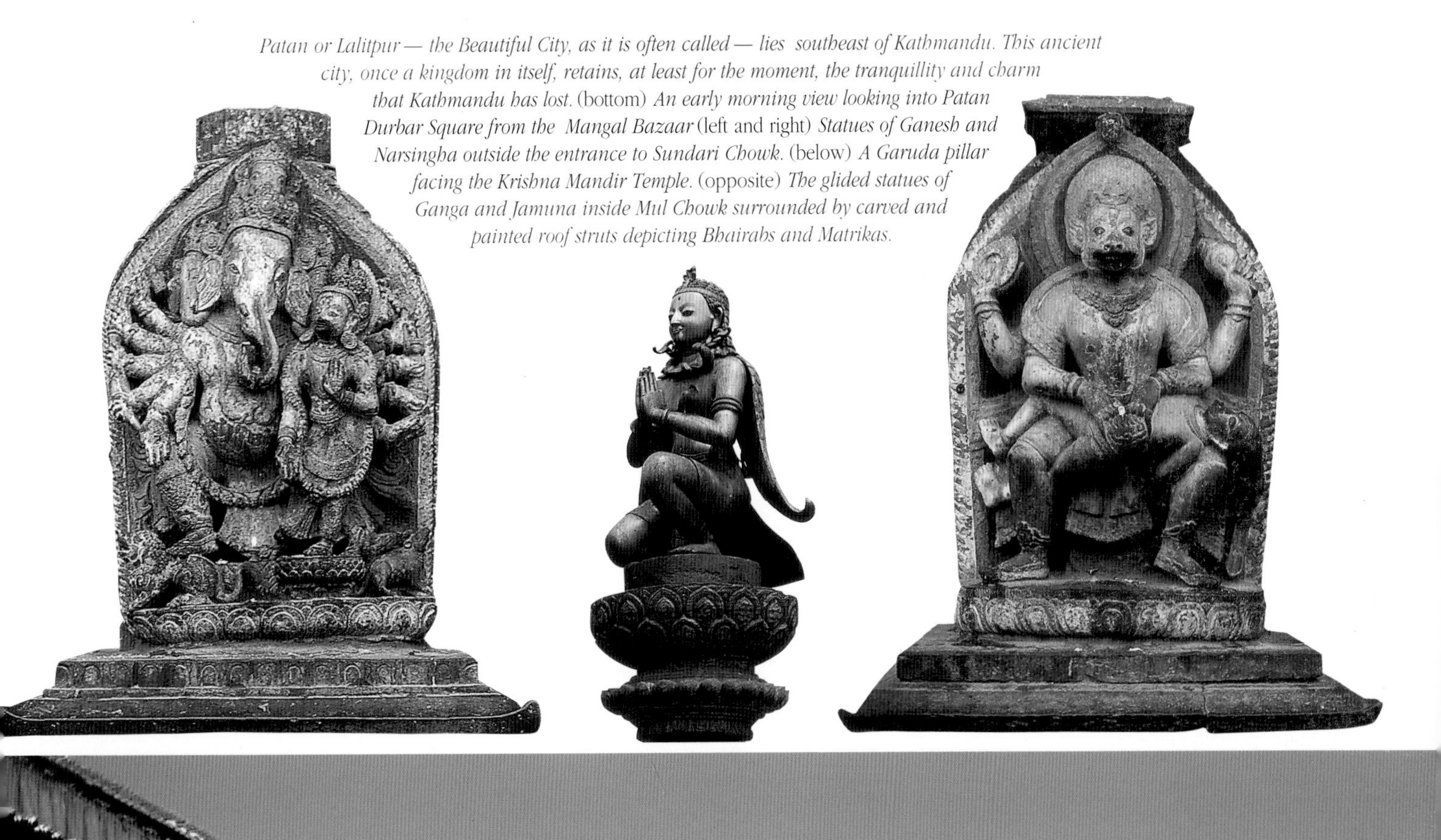

Patan or Lalitpur — the Beautiful City, as it is often called — lies southeast of Kathmandu. This ancient city, once a kingdom in itself, retains, at least for the moment, the tranquillity and charm that Kathmandu has lost. (bottom) *An early morning view looking into Patan Durbar Square from the Mangal Bazaar* (left and right) *Statues of Ganesh and Narsingha outside the entrance to Sundari Chowk.* (below) *A Garuda pillar facing the Krishna Mandir Temple.* (opposite) *The glided statues of Ganga and Jamuna inside Mul Chowk surrounded by carved and painted roof struts depicting Bhairabs and Matrikas.*

(above) *The Krishna Mandir.* (left and below) *Several examples of fine stone animal carvings to be seen throughout Patan Durbar Square.* (right) *A Newar woman making flower garlands used for worship or to honour a person.* (bottom right) *Souvenir stalls outside the Vishwanath Temple.*

(opposite) *Samples of the many delicate gilded wooden carvings and metalwork to be found in Patan Durbar Square and a view of the two elephants guarding the Vishwanath Temple silhouetted through the wooden supports of a public resthouse.*

(top and above) *Terracotta relief images of tiny Buddhas adorn the Shikara-style temple of Mahabuddha, with its main tower* (top). (right) *Finely carved windows in south Patan and necklaces of corn garland a small temple north of Patan.*

(opposite) *Details of delicate stone carvings adorning many of the monuments in Patan Durbar Square.*

(opposite) *Scenes in the vicinity of Patan.* (bottom three pictures) *The Mata-ya or Procession of Lights which is one of Patan's popular festivals. It involves a day-long procession of devotees who visit all the main Buddhist temples. Some devotees wear elaborate costumes and traditional musical bands also take part in the parade.* (this page) *Strange metal mythic beasts, prayer wheels and a monkey in the courtyard of the Golden Temple, or Kwa Bahal in Newari. Unlike many of Patan's* bahal, *Kwa Bahal is still actively supported, the monastery was founded in 1409 and is dedicated to the Gautama Buddha.*

The metalwork in the Golden Temple, especially the toranas, *is very detailed and finely executed. The small shrine in the centre of the courtyard is lavishly embellished with metal designs and figures, all of which merit a closer look.* (opposite far middle) *A scribe diligently copies a religious text.*

There are many means of transport ranging from public buses to minibuses, to taxis to scooters, the three-wheeled tempos (above top), *to rickshaws to bicycles, or a popular means of travel — by foot! The roads in Kathmandu are becoming increasingly congested, noisy and polluted with the vast majority of Nepal's vehicles crammed into the Valley. In 1999 the government did ban the larger six to eight seat* tempos (below) *from the city and has a long term programme to replace all the small internal combustion engined* tempos *with non-polluting electric versions* (right). *Taxis are aneasy and reasonably priced way to get around the city. Be prepared for a lot of walking, both in the towns and out in the countryside. The next best thing to walking is to take a rickshaw — the slow-moving, bell-ringing, brightly coloured local transport.*

BA.A.CHA 9146
SAFA TEMPO
NEPAL ELECTRIC VEHICLE INDUSTRY
Ph. - 415034
A NON-POLLUTING
ELECTRIC VEHICLE

CRAFTS

uel®
pal's Favourite
No.(1) 3000. Lt.
शुभ यात्रा
स्वागतम
TATA

Kathmandu is full of street vendors selling everything from spices to lottery tickets, as well as vegetables, coconuts, newspapers, flutes, soft drinks and cigarettes.

SPICES TEA
BEST CARDAMON TEA
BEST GREEN TEA
SAFFRON
PURE SAFFRON
Fish & Prawn Masala
Meat Masala
Garlic Powder
Garam Masala
Chicken Curry Masala
Hot Curry Masala
Mild Curry Masala

The old bazaar area runs from the Kasthamandap resthouse where the old trade route to Tibet began and then through Durbar Square to Indra Chowk. Make a point to wander through this permanently crowded and fascinating area, which always has something to watch, and occasionally even something to buy. Most of the goods on sale are daily necessities. Many of the shops have finely carved pillars and woodwork, and many are so small the shopkeeper can reach every item without moving from his cross-legged position.

Coca-Cola

The Valley is heaven for seasonal vegetables — immense cauliflowers, carrots, eggplants, beans and cabbages in the winter; peppers, peas, tomatoes, spinach, and lettuce in the spring; squash, cucumbers and many local vegetables without English names during the monsoon season. The situation with fruit is not so good but excellent apples are grown in the northern regions of Nepal.

Religion is the wellspring of traditional Nepali life, inspiring art, defining culture, and regulating daily routines. The multiple gods reflect the many facets of human nature. They dwell in temples, rocks or stones, mountains, trees, rivers, in the rafters, windows and hearths of houses, and most of all in the hearts and minds of the devotees. A Valley day begins with worship of the household deities followed by a visit to the neighbourhood temples.

The essential rite of worship is puja, *offerings meant to please the divine senses. Devotees scatter flower blossoms, uncooked rice and red tika powder on statues,* agams *and* lingams, *light oil lamps and incense, and ring temple bells to alert the gods to their presence. Coloured powder is also used during the Holi festival, or the festival of colour. It is a week of fun and revelry, especially among the young, who shower everybody with coloured water and powder. Nobody is safe, so be sure to wear old clothes if you venture out during Holi.*

Kathmandu offers an abundance of unique shopping. The sheer quantity of prayer wheels, statues, woodcarving, thangkas, *delicate jewellery, silverware, carpets, textiles, antiques, ornate* khukris, *puppets, baseball hats and the amazing array of masks can be overwhelming.*

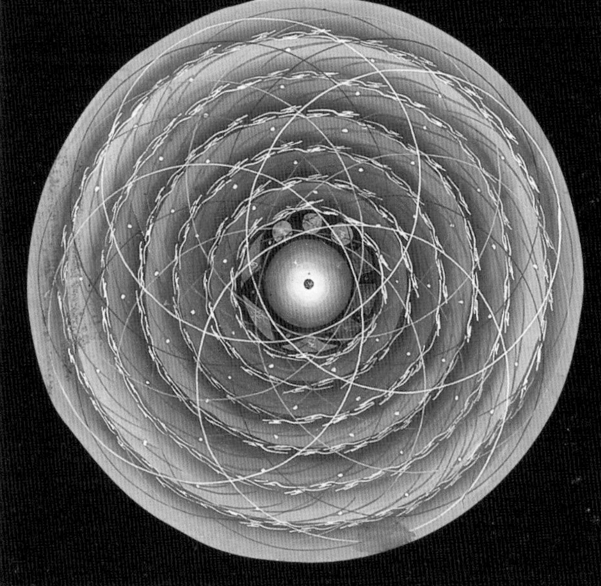

EVEREST BOOK SERVICE
BOOKSELLERS. AGENTS & DISTRIBUTORS.
P.O.BOX-2121, JAMAL, KATHMANDU.
OPEN
Everest Book Service
Birds Books
Trekking Guide
POST CARDS
NEWS PAPER
NEPALI PHOTOS

CHITWAN National Park
WILDLIFE RESERVE
NAGARKOT
KATHMANDU VALLEY
LHASA
SKY OF NEPAL
GOKYO
KHUMBU
LANTANG
LOWER DOLPO
GHANDRUNG
RARA JUMLA
ROLPA
NUWAKOT
MANASLU
HELAMBU
NEPA MAPS
チベット
MOUNT EVEREST
MUKTINATH JOMOSOM
GOSAINKUND
Nepal
ROUND ANNAPURNA
MANASLU GANESH HIMAL
KHUMBU
ROUND ANNAPURNA

Every face tells a story.

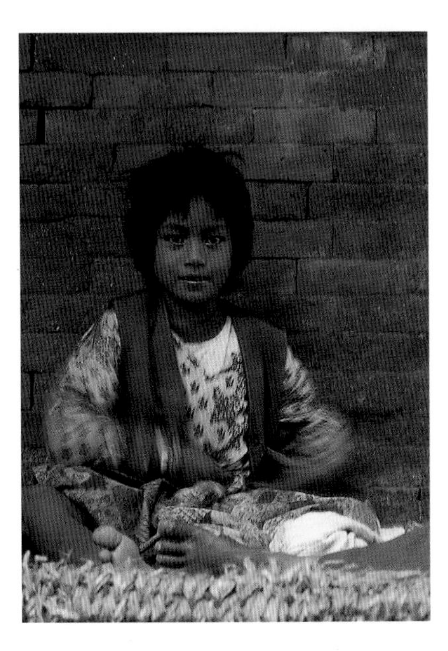

Sadhu, or Hindu holy men wander the Valley on a perpetual barefoot pilgrimage to holy places. They are lean, fierce-eyed men who prowl the streets and temples with begging bowls. They belong to a millennia-old Hindu tradition of vagabond ascetics who renounce family and caste to follow Shiva, a subculture involving an intricate network of sects and traditions. A sadhu's affiliation can be interpreted by his garments, by the implements he carries, and by the coloured designs painted on his forehead. Some spend their lives performing austerities, refusing to lie down for years on end or surviving on a diet of milk. Like any other slice of humanity, the sadhu spans the full range of saints, sinners and rogues.

Just about every village family has a few goats and chickens. A cow or water buffalo is expensive to purchase, but supplies a small cash income from the sale of milk. The cow is Nepal's national animal and the symbol of fertility and prosperity. Cow worship is believed to have the power to nullify an unlucky horoscope and reaches its peak on the third day of the festival of Tihar, the festival of light, when wandering bovines are washed, fed and adorned with red tika *and garlands. Rhesus monkeys are a common sight at most temples and palaces where they climb all over the buildings and beg for food.*

(opposite) *Eyes used as a protective device to avert evil spirits adorn many doors.*

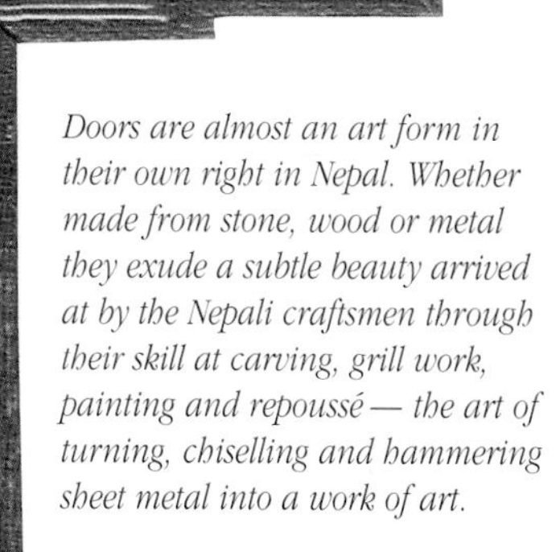

Doors are almost an art form in their own right in Nepal. Whether made from stone, wood or metal they exude a subtle beauty arrived at by the Nepali craftsmen through their skill at carving, grill work, painting and repoussé — the art of turning, chiselling and hammering sheet metal into a work of art.

Once the capital of the entire Valley, Bhaktapur is now the most isolated and unspoiled of the three former kingdoms. Its peaceful, yet busy streets, preserve nearly intact the medieval atmosphere of bygone days. (top left and right) *Two views of Bhaktapur Durbar Square.* (above) *King Malla's Pillar.* (left and right) *Statues of Bhairab and Durga.* (below left) *A side view of the guesthouse looking back to the main square.* (below) *The Golden Gate.* (below right) *A beautiful* lingam *seen through a small door in the guesthouse.*

(opposite top left) *Pairs of splendid guardians lining the steps to the sanctuary of the Bhagvati Temple.* (far top right) *A majestic bronze guardian lion.* (right) *The bathing pool known as Nag Pokhari. This bathing courtyard was constructed in the early 17th century.* (far right) *The sunken pool and the gilded head of Vasuki, the snake god and a golden waterspout.*

The Gai Jatra, or Cow Festival is one of the more colourful festivals in the Valley. The festival involves a cow, or young children dressed as cows parading through the towns as a tribute to the recently deceased and to assist their entry into heaven. The festival is Nepal's equivalent of a Halloween parade.

In Kathmandu, the bereaved families proceed along the festival route individually. In Patan, the participants gather at Durbar Square and then move oft together. The celebration held in Bhaktapur, as illustrated here is by far the most interesting and is a riot of colour.

Tall bamboo poles, wrapped in cloth and ribbons and topped with horns made out of straw, are carried around the city.

The family procession starts after early morning prayers and winds around the city. During the afternoon the procession

takes on a more carnival-like atmosphere, when participants mimic and lampoon the social scene, government institutions, ministers, husbands and wives, or anything within reach.

The processions staged in Bhaktapur are the most extensive and amusing, with a wide range of tableaux typifying all aspects of the people and culture. The festival lasts for about eight days, with the first and second days being the most important.

On the second day of the festival in Patan, an important Buddhist festival known as Mataya also takes place, when all the viharas *(Buddhist monasteries or temples) are visited in sequence. As there are about 150 of them, this is a formidable undertaking. Offerings are made by the pilgrims and butter lamps are lit along the route.*

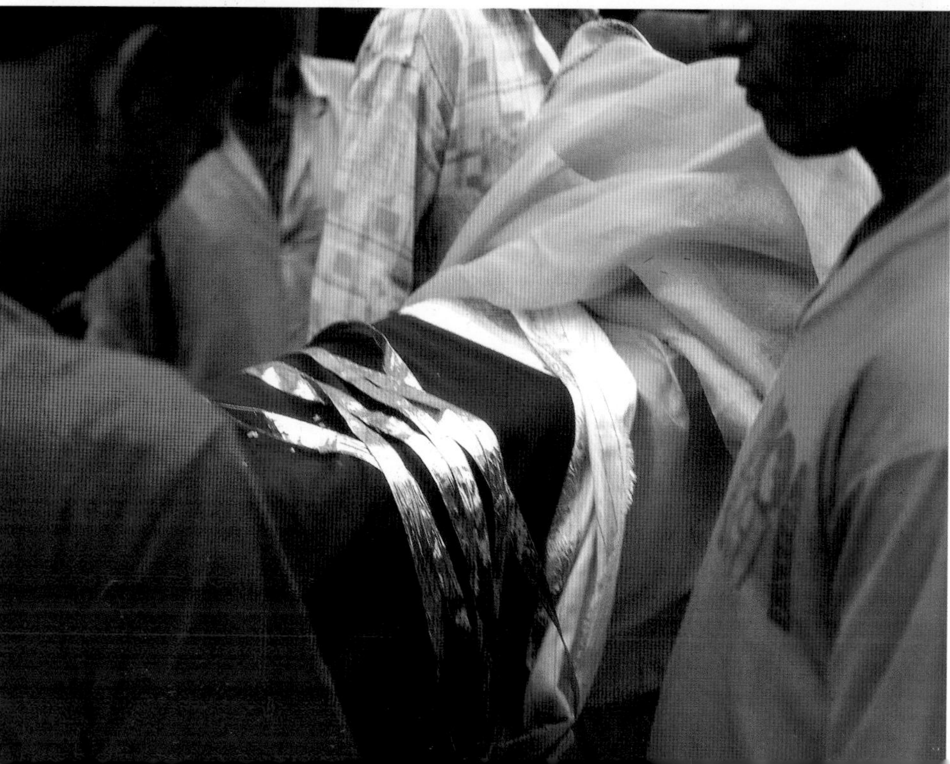

(left and below left) *A gilded window and the main shrine of the Kasi Biswanath Temple in Taumadhi Tol.* (above) *A guardian lion for the temple* (below). (opposite) *The Nyatapola Temple dominates Taumadhi Tol in Bhaktapur and, at 30 metres, is the tallest temple in Nepal.*

Perhaps the best-known craft in Nepal is the woodcarving that adorns both domestic and religious buildings. This craft reached its fullest developement among the Newari tribes in the 15th and 16th centuries, during the Malla rule. The royal palaces promoted local arts and some of the best examples of each period of woodcarving are found in the palace and temple complexes. Windows and floors are provided with a series of unique surrounds and mouldings. Cornices are built up of these basic shapes which are derived from heads, birds or vegetable and flower motifs. Each of these is a unique individual element. A splendid peacock spreads his intricately carved wooden tail from the famous "Peacock Window" (left) on Bhaktapur's Purjari Math. The elaborately carved building houses the National Art Gallery's Woodworking Museum.

Two views of the great Boudhanath Stupa with its all-seeing eyes that survey the four directions from its location east of Kathmandu.

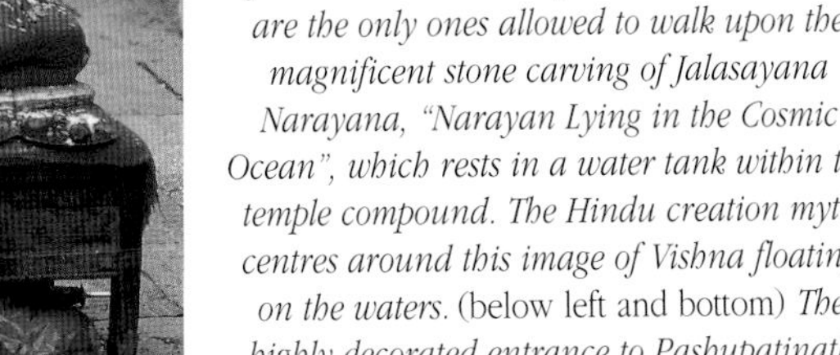

At the Hindu shrine of Budhanilkantha, north of Kathmandu, devotees come all day long, bringing offerings which the hand over to the yellow-clad Brahman priests. These votaries are the only ones allowed to walk upon the magnificent stone carving of Jalasayana Narayana, "Narayan Lying in the Cosmic Ocean", which rests in a water tank within the temple compound. The Hindu creation myth centres around this image of Vishna floating on the waters. (below left and bottom) *The highly decorated entrance to Pashupatinath and a ghostly tree silhouetted in a chilly morning mist.*

Changu Narayan is one of the earliest religious settlements in the Kathmandu Valley — a Hindu site of similar importance to the Buddhist one of Swayambhunath. Set on a rock peninsula running from the Nagakot range to the east, the temple is one of the most celebrated Vaishnava shrines of the Valley — its origin dates back to the fourth century, but probably earlier. It contains some glorious woodcarvings and metalwork, and the courtyard is a veritable museum of fine and ancient sculptures.

(following spread) *Pastoral landscapes like this characterise the Valley's countryside.*

Nepali life is based on farming. Agriculture supports over 80 percent of the population, with rice, wheat and maize as well as lentils, being the main staples. The hills and slopes of the Valley are coveredt top to bottom, in layers of terraced fields patiently carved out over the centuries with simple hand-held implements.

Set along the top of a ridge in the southwest of the Valley, the old Newar village of Kirtipur is a natural fortress, founded in the 12th century as an offshoot of Patan. (below) *A Brahmin ties a sacred yellow thread on the wrist of a boy during Janai Purnima or the Sacred Thread Festival.*

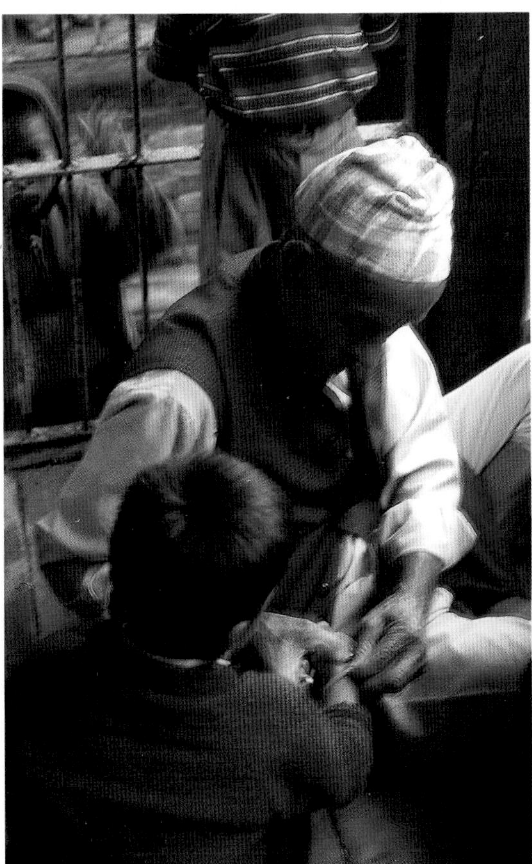

(left) *The beautiful gilt-copper roof of the 17th-century temple o Jal Binayak, one of the many shrines to Ganesh, is set on the ba of the Bagmati River just below the Chobar Gorge.* (top) *The gor is spanned by an old iron suspension bridge erected in 1907. A the parts were manufactured in Scotland, shipped to India an carried over the hills by lines of porters.* (below) *A temple pries deep in religious study.* (opposite) *Seventeen kilometres south o Kathmandu is the sacred sitee of Pharping, its clears pools of water surrounded by ancient stone sculptures and resthouses.*

Fascinating old relics are scattered around the many shrines at Pharping. Among the sacred temples are Shikar Narayan, one of the Valley's four main Vishnu sites, a temple dedicated to Vajra Yogini, and several Tibetan Buddhist monasteries.

Pharping draws both Hindus and Buddhists with its diverse combinations of sacred shrines, including an elaborate Tibetan Bhuddist chorten (left). Many of the temples and monuments are festooned with colourful prayer flags. All are skillfully intregated into the beatiful natural setting.

उद्गारवती

Set in a shaded grotto on the confluence of two small streams, Dakshinkali Temple is the Valley's most significant shrine to Kali, "The Black One." Scowling and emaciated, with a protruding tongue and red eyes, decked with a necklace of skulls, Kali is an aspect of Shiva's consort Durga, appearing in fearsome form to battle with evil. Placated with sacrificial offerings, she will readily bestow gifts and blessings and absolve sins. (following spread) *The mist rises with the heat of the early morning sun in Das Valley.*

(above, below and top right) *The village of Sankhu is a treasury of Newar architecture. Remaining dignified, many of its richly decorated old houses now sit at crooked angles or are crumbling. The pillars and pediments on the façades of some buildings demonstrate the Rana-era fascination with European opulence.* (below right) *The beautiful Varja Yogani Temple which is located on a hill a few kilometres north of Sankhu.* (following spread) *The truly magnificent view from the small hilltop resort of Nagakot on the Valley's northeast rim overlooking the central and eastern Himalayas.*

Selected Accommodation

There is a plethora of accommodation in Kathmandu, from rambling old Rana palaces to sleek modern highrises. Prices listed here are for a double room in high season, October-November, with a smaller surge in March-April. While top hotels may be booked solid at this time, there is never a lack of rooms. In the off-season, especially during the monsoon, rates can drop by as much as 50 percent. Room rates are negotiable in all but luxury hotels, where you simply request a business discount.

All but the cheapest hotels require payment in foreign currency, and state their rates in U.S. dollars. Government tax added to hotel bills ranges from 10 to 16 percent, according to the rating. The hotels listed here are rated according to the following categories:
Expensive: All the mod cons — shopping arcade, air-conditioned rooms (welcome in the summer months), top-class restaurants, and often a swimming pool and/or tennis courts. Prices run from US$100-$155 for a double room.
Moderate: Hotels in this category are smaller but often have a more creative ambience than the stodgy standards, while rooms may be the same quality, or even better. Prices range from US$40-$80 for a double.
Budget: dozens of budget hotels and lodges are clustered in Thamel. Quoted prices are around US$20 for a simple, but clean double room with minimal furniture, carpet, phone and bath, though room rates are always negotiable. Rock-bottom budget lodges on Freak Street charge as little as US$3 per day.

Things to look for in a hotel: character, quiet and location (you should take full advantage of Kathmandu's walkability, and there's nothing worse than a hotel you have to beg taxi drivers to take you to late at night). The big difficulty is finding a room with character. Even luxury hotels tend to have small, unimaginatively decorated rooms, often redolent of monsoon mildew. Some of the more out-of-the-way places reward their guests with extra charm. Only the most expensive hotels have heating and air conditioning —all the more reason to choose a place with a big garden or rooftop terrace where you can soak up the sun or relax in the shade. Accommodation outside Kathmandu is generally much simpler. All towns of note have local inns, though the signboard may be only in Nepali. Usually the noise level is high, and cleanliness (and prices) low.

Kathmandu

Expensive

Hotel Yak & Yeti, Durbar Marg (tel. 222-635). The best luxury hotel in Kathmandu: centrally located, it combines all the amenities with a touch of class — one wing is housed in an old Rana palace.
Hotel de l'Annapurna, Durbar Marg (tel. 221-711). Good location but slightly dingy rooms; great swimming pool.
Hotel Soaltee Holiday Inn Crowne Plaza, Tahachal (tel. 273999, 272-555). Kathmandu's largest hotel. Notable restaurants and mountain views compensate somewhat for the inconvenient location.
Everest Hotel, New Baneswor (tel. 220-567). Formerly the Sheraton. Good rooms, some with mountain views, but again inconveniently located.
Hotel Himalayas, Kopundol, Lalitpur (tel. 523-900). On the road to Patan, with fantastic mountain views on clear days; ask for a room facing the garden.
Hotel Malla, Lainchaur (tel. 410-320). Well-situated just north of Thamel, this hotel is quiet, with a pleasant lobby and gardens.
Hotel Shangri-la, Lazimpat (tel. 412-999). Rooms are simple but ambience and service superb. Built around a wonderful garden with a swimming pool modeled after the traditional sunken fountains. Good restaurants, reasonably well-located.
Hotel Shanker, Lazimpat (tel. 410-151). The white stucco exterior of this hotel, an old Rana palace, is a baroque fantasy. Rooms are less than palatial, but at least they have character. Sweeping gardens, good location.
Hotel Sherpa, Durbar Marg (tel. 227-102). Great location, rooms a bit cramped, but all the amenities at a reasonable price.
Radisson Hotel Kathmandu, Lazimpat, (tel, 411-818, 423-888). Located adjacent to the Royal Palace. With eight floors offering great views of the surrounding mountains.

Moderate

Hotel Vajra, Bijeswori (tel. 272-545). A unique compendium of local culture, starting with the red-brick buildings set with woodcarvings and tiled roofs. Other attractions include gardens, a Finnish sauna, and an active cultural scene including traditional dance performances, an art gallery, and a well-stocked library run by a genuine swami. The biggest drawback is location — it's not close to anything but Swayambhunath, and it's a 15-minute walk into Thamel. Rooms range from US$15-$80.
Hotel Marsyangdi, Paknajol, Thamel (tel. 414-105). This six-storey hotel even boasts an elevator, a distinct step up from the usual Thamel lodgings. Very nicely decorated rooms, some with air-con and TV, with views improving the higher you go.

Hotel Thamel, Thamel (tel. 417-643). Another new highrise with decent rooms, many with balconies, and a rooftop garden.
Hotel Sunset View, New Baneswar (tel. 229-172). Across from the Everest Hotel, this Thakali-run hotel has a Japanese garden with views of the city, an excellent Japanese restaurant, and bright, airy, large rooms.
Kantipur Temple House, Jyatha Tol, Thamal (tel. 250-131). Built in the style of a Newari Temple. Cosy restaurant and a roof-top terraced garden offering views of the Royal Palace.
Summit Hotel, Kopundol Heights (tel. 521-810). Set on a bluff overlooking the city, this hotel features traditional architecture in a lush garden setting, complete with a small pool. Rooms are simple and traditionally decorated. Location is the drawback — it's not really walking distance to anywhere.
Dwarika's Kathmandu Village Hotel, Battisputali (tel. 470-770). Definitely something special. The buildings are in traditional Newari style and incorporate old woodcarvings; the newly renovated rooms are furnished with similar attention to traditional detail. On the east side of town, near Pashupatinath.

BUDGET

Kathmandu Guest House, Thamel (tel. 413-632). The place that started the Thamel boom back in the early 70s, the Kathouse has become a legend in its own time, supported by a world-traveller clientele. Nice lobby and garden, located in the heart of Thamel. Room rates vary according to wing, from US$8-$35 double, with discounts for long-term stays.
Mustang Holiday Inn, Jyatha, Thamel (tel. 226-538). Clean and exceptionally pleasant rooms in a range of prices, set back from the Thamel fray.
Hotel Garuda, Paknajol, Thamel, (tel. 416-776). Pleasant atmosphere, scrupulously clean rooms, some with small balconies, a rooftop terrace and friendly staff make this small place exceptionally good value.

Tibet Guesthouse, Thamel (tel. 214-383). A favourite with mountaineers and return visitors; friendly and clean, with a rooftop garden.
Hotel Shri Tibet, Thamel (tel. 419-902). A homey little place with Tibetan decor on a quiet lane.
International Guesthouse, Kaldhara (tel. 410-533). Another homey place, this is actually a house — a very nice, large modern one — serving as a hotel. A good location if you want to escape Thamel yet still be within walking distance.
Hotel Shakti, Thamel (tel. 410-121) Set back from the thick of the Thamel scene, with one wing in an old Rana palace, the Shakti is a quiet refuge with some exceptionally cheap rooms.
Hotel Manaslu, Lazimpat (tel. 410-071). A well-maintained hotel on the north side of town, with large rooms and a big sunny garden.
Stupa Hotel, Boudhanath (tel. 470-385). Five kilometres east of Kathmandu, the largely Tibetan community of Boudhanath offers a quiet alternative to the city. Friendly staff at this reasonable hotel.
Dragon Guesthouse, Boudhanath (tel. 479-562). Friendly, clean, and very cheap guesthouse with a family atmosphere.
Hotel Zenith, Patan Dhoka (tel. 522-932). At last a reasonable alternative in Patan. This new and well-maintained hotel has a restaurant, garden, and even e-mail service.
For rock-bottom prices (less than US$2 for a room with common bath) try **Kathmandu Lodge** and **Kumari Lodge** off Durbar Square, **Lodge Pheasant** and **Cosy Corner** in Thamel, or **Peace Guesthouse** in Tahachal.

BHAKTAPUR

Bhaktapur Guesthouse, Chundevi (tel. 610-670). This simple hotel set atop a peaceful hill overlooking fields is a half-hour stroll from town, on the south side of the Bhaktapur road past the turnoff.
Bhadgaun Guesthouse, Taumadhi Tol (tel. 610-488). Nice rooms, some with views, and a rooftop restaurant, in this, the best of Bhaktapur's modest budget guesthouses.
Golden Gate Guest House, (tel. 610-534). A simple place: best is the upstairs room, with big windows overlooking Durbar Square.

NAGARKOT

The Farmhouse, (tel. 228-087 or through Hotel Vajra, 272-719). Run by the Hotel Vajra, this converted old farmhouse features tiled floors, brick-and-wood decor, and a pretty garden with prayer flags and stupa. There are four rooms with shared bath in the main building, four with separate bath in a new wing. By far the classiest place to stay in Nagarkot — though not necessarily the fanciest. Moderate rates include meals.
Niva Hotel, (tel. 290-797). New and elegant rooms and a lovely terrace, all well-maintained by Japanese management. Expensive.
Peaceful Cottage, (tel. 290-877). Among the better places in central Nagarkot, with largish rooms and a spacious terrace. Budget.
Green Peace Horizon, Very simple and quiet in a row of tiny bamboo huts perched on the edge of a dizzying view. Budget.

Recommended Restaurants

For an isolated Himalayan country, Kathmandu's tourist restaurants offer an amazing variety of cuisines. Cost in even the most expensive hotel restaurants is low: it's difficult for even a fancy dinner to top Rs800 unless you indulge in expensive imported liquor.

The best prepared food is Indian cuisine, featuring highly spiced meat and vegetable dishes served with rice or flat bread and an array of condiments. Go with a group of friends and

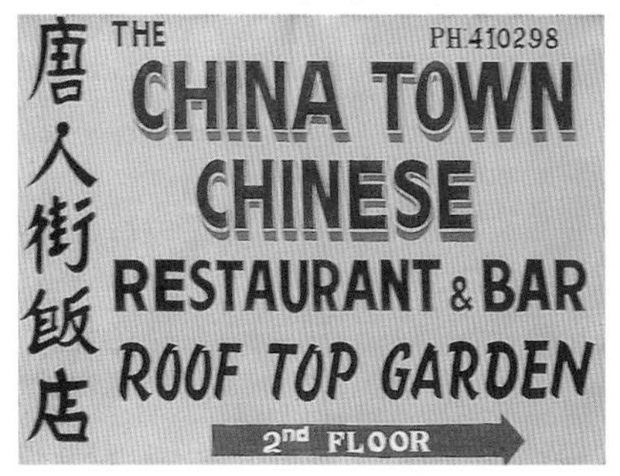

order together to maximise choice: try tandoori chicken (roasted in a clay oven), chewy warm naan (flat bread), curried vegetables, rice, dal, and a cooling raita (yoghurt sauce). For an intensely sweet finish sample almond-flavoured gulab jamun or cardomon-spiked rasmalai. The bravest should conclude with paan, a mixture of spices and crushed betel nut wrapped in a leaf and chewed for a mildly intoxicating effect. Sold in tiny street stalls, it stains the teeth a gory red.

Budget tourist restaurants in Thamel and Freak Street have wholeheartedly embraced foreign cuisine, with the mixed results which can be expected from menus offering Mexican, Italian, French, American and Chinese food all in the same breath. Dishes are palatable, but too often everything tastes the same. Still, Rs80 will bring a large and nourishing meal. Set breakfasts are an especially good deal: eggs, toast, potatoes and coffee/tea for Rs50. Cakes and pies are another specialty left over from the days of Asian overland travellers; some are excellent, others rely on large portions rather than flavour.

Locals eat at home, or at bhojnalaya or small hole-in-the-wall eateries dishing up snacks, simple food and homemade raksi. Chinese and Indian restaurants are good choices if you're entertaining Nepali guests, and plenty of restaurants have combination Chinese-Indian-Continental menus to please everyone in a large group.

Kathmandu

Indian

Bangalore Coffee House, Jamal (just off Durbar Marg). For the adventurous, a local eatery featuring cheap South Indian vegetarian food. Try the dosa, a crispy pancake of lentil flour stuffed with spicy vegetables.

Ghar-E-Kabab, Durbar Marg. Acclaimed as Kathmandu's best restaurant, though there are many others just as good. Certainly it serves excellent food at a reasonable price, with the added entertainment of watching the chefs skewer kebabs and flatten naan behind a glass window. The ghazal singing is good but obtrusive enough to ruin dinnertime conversation.

Moti Mahal or The Amber, Durbar Marg. Local versions of the Ghar-e-Kabab, complete with lower-volume ghazal music and glassed-in kitchens. Food is quite good and much cheaper.
Naachghar, Hotel Yak & Yeti, Durbar Marg. Rich Indian vegetarian food served in a stunning palatial setting: crystal chandeliers, marble floors, fluted pillars, and music nightly.

Nepali/Tibetan

Bhanchha Ghar, Kamaladi. Delicious upscale Nepali cuisine, far different than what you'll find on the trail: spiced boar, mushroom curry, and tiny clay cups of the incendiary house raksi. Set in a renovated old farmhouse, with an interesting bar on the top floor.
Bhojan Griha, Dillibazar. An old historic building which has been restored. Traditional folk music and dance performances each evening.
Dechen Ling, Thamel. Momos, thukpa and other Tibetan standards.
Kathmandu Kitchen, Seto Durbar Gate, Durbar Marg. Nepali cuisine in the Kathmandu Valley style.
Nepali Kitchen, Thamel. A budget version of the above, serving reasonably priced Nepali food (a Continental menu too) in a pleasant garden courtyard.
Thamel House, Thamel. Elegantly situated in a restored old Newar house in North Thamel, with set meals and a la carte ordering as well.

Mixed Cuisine

Nanglo, Durbar Marg. This conveniently located rooftop terrace serving Continental food and tasty dal bhat is popular with both tourists and locals.
Saino, just off Durbar Marg and near the Royal Palace. Pleasant outdoor and indoor dining with the usual multicultural menu (Indian, Chinese, Tibetan, Continental). A good place for drinks and snacks.
Shambhala Garden Cafe, Shangri-La Hotel, Lazimpat. The only 24-hour restaurant in town, with a daily breakfast buffet and dining on the portico overlooking the lovely garden. Bhaktapur Night, held here Fridays in tourist season, features costumed dancers and an elaborate buffet in the torchlit garden (reservations tel. 412-999).
Sunrise Restaurant, the Yak & Yeti, Durbar Marg. Hotel coffee shop with an Asian/ Continental menu and an evening buffet.

The Bakery Café, Kamaladi, New Road, and Jawalakhel. A local chain serving fast food in a sit down setting.
Wunjala Moskva, Naxal. Serving both Newari, and as the name suggests Russian food.

Western

Al Fresco, Hotel Soaltee Holiday Inn, Tahachal. The best Italian food in town, in an airy trattoria-type setting.
Chimney Room, Hotel Yak and Yeti, Durbar Marg. The menu includes Chicken Kiev, steaks, lobster, and borscht, but you should come mainly for the ambience and history of this restaurant, started by legendary hotelier Boris Lissanevitch. The red-brick room built around a copper-chimneyed fireplace is cosiest in winter.
Everest Steakhouse, Thamel. The place for carnivores.
Fire & Ice, Thamel. Across from Immigration, this wildly popular place serves superb pizzas and ice cream.
Gourmet Deli/Old Vienna, Thamel. Order breakfast and sandwiches at the deli counter, or dine in the restaurant on stolid Austrian food. An excellent source for picnic fare.
Gurkha Grill, Hotel Soaltee Holiday Inn, Tahachal. Excellent Continental restaurant; some vegetarian dishes too, plus music and dancing.

K.C.'s, Thamel., Balajutar. An old Newari farmhouse transformed into an unusual and elegant retreat. Dine indoors in a traditionally decorated setting or out on the peaceful garden terrace. Great for kids, as there's a playground and staff to supervise.
K.C.'s, Thamel. A cut above the usual Thamel standard, known for its pizza, fettucine, sizzling steaks and baked potatoes.
Le Bistro, Thamel. Old standby with budget travellers enamoured of its generously portioned meat and vegetarian dishes and fantastic chocolate cake.
Mike's Breakfast, Naxal (take the road curving north from Nag Pokhari). The place to meet your friends in the sunny garden for breakfast and lunch (dinner is served too, in all but the coldest months). Brewed coffee, fresh bread, sandwiches, soups and salads, and Mexican food.
Northfield Café, Thamel. All the Mike's standards in an equally pleasant setting.
Simply Shutters, Babar Mahal Revisited. An elegant bistro in an equally elegant new shopping centre.
Stupa View, Boudhanath. The Austrian vegetarian food is tolerable, or order cappuccino and apple strudel and enjoy the views from the rooftop terrace.

SANDWICHES AND TAKEAWAY

Delicatessen Center, Kanti Path. The largest deli in Kathmandu, selling various cheeses and cold cuts.

Hot Breads, Durbar Marg and Thamel. Fresh baked goods, both sweet and savoury. Also solid and cheap breakfasts.
Nirula's, Durbar Marg. Awful fast food, but 24 flavours of ice cream.
Pumpernickel German Bakery, Thamel. Cheap, simple fare — sandwiches, eggs, pastries, coffee — in a garden that's a favourite with young world travellers. Also rolls, bagels and croissants for takeout.
Shangri-La Bakery, Lazimpat. The best pastries in town, plus bread, cakes and coffee.

JAPANESE

Fuji, Kanti Path. Food is so-so, but the setting is unbeatable: an old Rana concubine's cottage, surrounded by a moat.
Koto, Durbar Marg and Thamel. Best deal is the set menu *bento*: miso soup to green tea and everything in between.
Kushi-Fuji, Durbar Marg. A good selection of sukiyaki, tempura and teriyaki.
Tamura, Thapatali Heights (tel. 526-732). Hard to find — there's not even a sign — but this exquisitely decorated authentic Japanese restaurant is worth the effort. Call for directions.

THAI

Baan Thai, Durbar Marg. Excellent Thai food, fairly expensive for Kathmandu.
Him Thai, Lazimpat. Again, the Thai food is not so convincing, but the outdoor garden is peaceful and usually empty.
Krua Thai, Thamal. A large restaurant with decor imported from Thailand.
Yin Yang, Thamel. Decent food in an elegant (for Thamel) setting with indoor and outdoor dining.

CHINESE

China Town, Lazimpat. Located above the Bluebird Supermarket, with good food and fast service.
Mei Hua, Kanti Path. A roomy local restaurant serving good cheap Chinese food, including *baozi*, hot-and-sour soup, and *jiaotzi*.
Thamal China Town, Thamal. A large restaurant with three floors with a terrace and a balcony.

Patan

Base Camp Café, Hotel Himalayas, Kopundol. Standard hotel coffee shop with splendid mountain views on clear days.
Cafe Pagode, Patan Durbar Square. Rooftop views of ancient temples, and decent basic fare.
German Bakery, Jawalakhel (near the zoo). Sandwiches, cakes, coffee and tea.
Museum Café, Patan Durbar. The food is simple, but the setting — a garden courtyard in the old palace complex — is sublime.
Summit Hotel, Kopundol Heights. All the ordinary fare, plus good Friday night barbecues. Sunday and Wednesdays feature an organic produce market followed by a multi-course vegetarian lunch.
Three Sisters Italian Restaurant, Phulchowk, Italian and other innovative dishes in this unusual restaurant.

Bhaktapur

Cafe Nyatapola, Taumadhi Tol. Food is rather unremarkable, but who can resist sitting in a real old pagoda complete with woodcarvings, overlooking the temples of Taumadhi Square.
Marco Polo, Tamaudhi Tol. Marginally better food, and a balcony with views.
Peacock Restaurant, Dattatreya Square. Situated in an elaborately carved old math overlooking another splendid square.

Nagarkot

The Teahouse. Nicely decorated building with indoor and outdoor dining and a menu featuring Indian and Nepali food.
Van Van, Hotel Niwa. A short menu of Japanese food, simple but well-prepared, and a lovely terrace plus indoor dining.

TRAVEL AGENTS

Ama Travel
Bhagwanbahal, Thamel, tel. 425-811, 423-431, fax. 248-493
Annapurna Travels & Tours
Kashmiri Takiya, Durbar Marg, tel. 222-339, 223-763, fax. 222-966
B-Line Travel & Tours
Kathmandu Plaza, tel. 223-477, 253-140, fax. 222-622
Blue Bird Travel & Tours
Thamel, tel. 425-719, 425-799, fax. 412-897

Broadway Travels
Naghpokhari (behind Royal Palace), tel. 412-656, fax. 425-125
Council Travel & Tours
Hattisar, tel. 437-539
Devi International Travel & Tours
Thamel, tel. 422-377, 425-924, fax. 410-079
Eco Tourist Service
Thamel, tel. 416-952, 424-074, fax. 420-532
Everest Travel Service
Kantipath, 249-216, 249-263, fax. 226-795
Geo Tours Nepal
Thamel, tel. 417-511, fax. 424-468, 260-763
Gorkha Vision Travel & Tours
Thamel Chowk, tel. 410-337, 263-698, fax. 423-011
Green Hill Tours, Treks & Expeditions
Northern Gate of Royal Palace, tel. 428-326, fax. 419-985
GSA Universal Tours & Travel
Kantipath, tel. 252-048, 252-049, fax. 220-267
Hard Rock Travel & Tours
Thamel, tel. 260-885, fax. 262-767
Heritage Tours & Travels
Katnipath (near British Council), tel. 246-781, fax. 241-820
Himalayan Holidays Tours & Travels
Gairidhara, tel. 428-756, 410-482, fax. 415-669
Himalayan Travels & Tours
Durbar Marg, tel. 223-045, 226-011, fax. 224-001
Himal Reisen
Thamel, tel. 426-913, fax. 419-186

Kamala Travels & Tours
Thamel. tel. 240-675, 226-466, fax. 232-065
Kanjiroba Travels & Tours
Thamel, tel. 227-882, fax. 250-046
Kathmandu Experience Travel & Tours
Maitighar, tel. 255-763, 255-747, fax. 227-521
Kathmandu - Lhasa Tours & Travel
Jyatha, Thamel, tel. 231-060, fax. 240-220
Kathmandu Travel & Tours
Battissputali, tel. 471-577, 493-218, fax. 471-379
Kohinoor Travels
Naxal, Hattisar, tel. 434-683, 435-686, fax. 430-686
Link Travel & Tours
Jyoti Niwas, Tripureswor, tel. 230-318, 242-351, fax. 248-214
Lost Horizon Travels & Tours
Yak & Yeti Plaza, tel. 247-703, 229-079, fax. 350-204
Manjushree Travel & Tours
New Road, tel. 223-574, 227-162, fax. 227-644
Mendo Travels & Tours
Gairidhara, tel. 437-986, 437-987, fax. 438-262
Muktinath Travel & Tours
Thamel, tel. 253-228, 256-656, fax. 253-215

Namaste Travels
Maitighar, tel. 225-405, 227-484, fax. 226-590
Natraj Tours & Travel
Kamaladi, tel. 222-906, 222-532, fax. 227-372
Nepal East West Travels & Tours
Freak Street, Jhochhen, tel. 223-831, 225-060, fax. 223-573
Nepal Kaze Travel
Tel. 240-393, 223-194, fax. 249-133
Nepal Sagarmatha Travels
Seto Durbar, tel. 225-471, 220-560, fax. 220-514
Oriental Travel & Tours
Kathmandu Plaza, tel. 246-390, 243-880, fax. 243-786
Pagoda Travel & Tours
Basantpur, tel. 252-226, 225-266, fax. 247-113
Panas Travel
Nagpokhari, Naxal, tel. 412-534, 414-718, fax. 429-273
Plan Holidays Travel & Tours
Tel. 423-599, 423-758, fax. 420-010
Potala Travels
Laldurbar, Kamaladi, tel. 222-350, 222-082, fax. 258-395
President Travels & Tours
Durbar Marg, tel. 220-245, 221-774, fax. 221-180

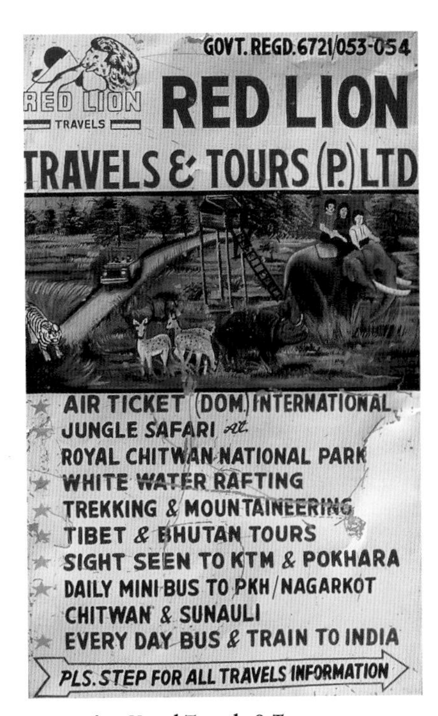

Promotion Nepal Travels & Tours
Kaldhara, tel. 266-138, fax. 419-625
Quality Travel Service
Naghpokhari-1, tel. 411-961, 414-746, fax. 430-758
Raaika Tours & Travels
Siddhu Niwas, Durbar Marg, tel. 434-476, 434-934, fax. 434-934
Rath Nepal Tours & Travel
Nag Pokhari, Naxal, tel. 425-323, 437-129, ax. 434-821
Red Lion Travels & Tours
Thamel, tel. 257-343, 260-595, fax. 257-343
Rhino Travel Agency
Thamel, tel. 416-300, 416-918, 420-316, fax. 417-146
Sakura Tours & Treks
Lazimpat, tel. 420-032, fax. 415-088
Savana Travel & Tours
Kasmiri Takiya, Durbar Marg, tel. 220-714, 231-749, fax. 221-351
Sea & Sky Tours & Travels
Thamel, tel. 264-593, fax. 227-314
Shangri-La Holidays & Tours of Enchantment
Lazimpat, tel. 415-283, 415-754, fax. 419-872, 420-239
Shangri-La Tours
Tel. 226-138, 226-139, fax. 227-068
Shashi's Holidays
Rani Pokhari, Jamal, tel. 227-018, 248-255, fax. 228-868

Shiva Kailash Tours
Baluwatar, tel. 412-334, 420-789, fax. 419-704
Sita World Travel (Nepal)
Tridevi Marg, tel. 418-363, 418-738, fax. 227-557
Tibet Travels & Tours
Tridevi Marg, tel. 249-140, 250-611, fax. 249-986
Tika Travel & Tours
Kantipath, tel. 226-189, fax. 246-834
Travelink Asia
Tridevi Marg, tel. 424-068, 429-322, fax. 423-331
Travel Net International
Naxal, tel. 418-910, fax. 429-437
Travel Planner
Bagbazar, tel. 225-674, 253-345, fax. 245-978
Trinity Travels
Kamaladi, tel. 222-160, 246-367, fax. 245-573
Trishakti Travel Agency
New Road, tel. 266-368, 266-379, fax. 266-379
Vascodigama Travels & Tours
Thamel, Narsingh Camp Gate, tel. 259-735, 264-855, fax. 263-149
Yeti Travels
Durbar Marg, tel. 221-234, 222-329, fax. 226-152
Ying Yang Travels
Thamel, tel. 423-358, 423-359, fax. 421-701, 414-653
Zen Travel & Tours
Tel. 415-260, 424-146, fax. 412-945

Trekking Agents

Adventure Country
Tel. 250-440, 250-441, fax. 425-657
Amadablam Adventure Group
Kamal Pokhari, tel. 415-372, 415-373, fax. 416-029, 421-882
Annapurna Treks & Expeditions
Tel. 423-656, 428-768, fax. 423-492
A-One Trekking
Durbar Marg, tel. 267-792, fax. 267-740
Asian Holidays Trekking
Maharajgunj, Lohsal, Ring Road, tel. 374-161, 373-338, fax. 374-162
Asian Trekking
Thamel, tel. 415-506, fax. 411-878
Atalante Mountaineering & Trekking
Tel. 483-660, fax. 483-661
Axis Trek & Expedition
Tripureswor, tel. 262-126, fax. 261-465
Bon Voyage Trekking Agency & Travels
Thamel, Narsingh Camp, tel. 427-487, 266-114, fax. 416-835
Discover Himalayan Treks
Thamel Mall Complex, tel. 258-975, 258-976, fax. 527-218
Dolpa Treks & expeditions
Tel. 260-567, fax. 252-193, 253-227
Eco Trek
Thamel, tel. 420-490, 424-112, 424-113, fax. 413-118
Enjoy Treks
Sano Gaucharan, tel. 423-948, 429-252, fax. 412-527
Euro Treks & Expedition
Thamel, tel. 264-280, fax. 253-007
First Environmental Trekking
Thamel. tel. 417-343, 424-346, fax. 423-855
Glacier Safari Treks
Bhagwan Bahal. Thamel, tel. 412-116, 414-549, fax. 418-578
Global Himalayas Trek
Thamel, Nasingh Camp, tel. 419-288, fax. 228-496
Heritage Trekking
Kantipath (near British Council), tel. 249-476, 246-781, fax. 241-820

Highlander Treks & Expeditions
Thamel, tel. 243-158, 424-563, fax. 411-889
Himalayan Envpro Adventures
Tel. 422-910, 410-722, fax. 418-918
Himalayan Excursions
Gairidhara, tel. 418-119, 421-260, fax. 418-913
Himalayan Glacier Trekking
Thamel, tel. 421-780, fax. 228-623
Himalayan High Country Treks & Expeditions
Maharajgunj, Chakrapath Chowk, tel. 413-675, fax. 436-544
Himalayan Journeys
Kantipath, tel. 226-138, 226-139, fax. 227-068
Himlung Treks
Kantipath (next to British Council), tel. 258-596, fax. 258-597
Hyecho Adventure Trekking & Mountaineering
Siddhu Niwas, Durbar Marg, tel. 434-476, 434-934, fax. 434-934
International Adventures Treks & Expeditions
Thamel, tel. 220-664, 229-312, fax. 229-312
International Trekkers
Chabahil, tel. 371-397, 370-714, 371-537, fax. 371-561
Karnali Treks & Expeditions
Thamel. tel. 263-822, fax. 472-529
Khumbi-Ila Mountaineering & Trekking
tel. 483-660, 483-664, fax. 483-661

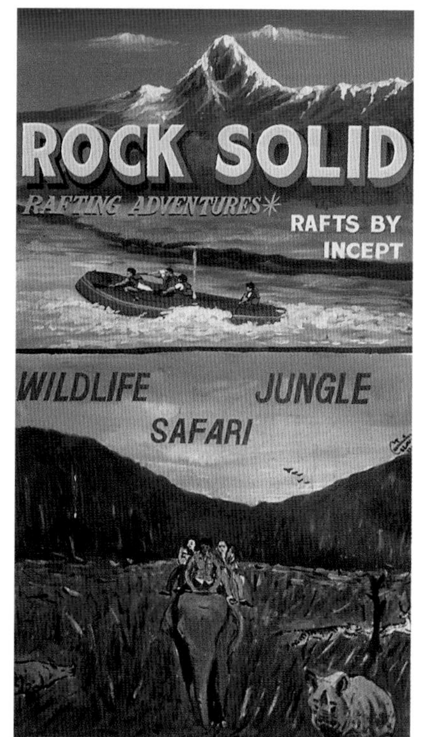

Lama Excursions
Chandol, Maharajgunj, tel. 425-812, 423-831, fax. 425-813
Lama Parivar Himalayan Treks
Thamel, tel. 423-612, 425-889, fax. 249-016
Langtang Ri Trekking
Thamel, tel. 424-268, 423-360, 423-586, fax. 424-267
Lomanthang Treks
Lazimpat, tel. 419-161, fax. 419-161
Lost Horizon Treks & Expeditions
Gairidhara, tel. 418-743, fax. 410-383
Marron Treks
Lazimpat, tel. 425-505, 425-747, fax. 418-088
Mendo Treks & Expeditions
Thamel, tel. 259-538, 258-412, fax. 258-419
Mountain Adventure Trekking
Jyatha, tel. 254-607, 250-061, fax. 525-126
Mount Makalu Trekking
Nagpokhari, Naya Bato, tel. 417-116, fax. 414-024
Mount Manaslu Adventure Treks
Thamel, tel. 423-542, 424-632, fax. 351-155
Multi Adventure
Tel. 257-791, fax. 257-792
Natraj Trekking
Kantipath, tel. 226-664, fax. 227-372
Nepal Himal Treks
Tel. 419-796, fax. 417-794
Nepal Myths & Mountain Trails
Sano, Gaucharan, tel. 429-894, fax. 429-674
Nepal Panorama Trek
Tel. 240-393, 223-194, fax. 249-133
Nepal Sanctuary Treks
Tel. 414-492, fax 429-520
Pabil Treks
Kamal Pokhari, tel. 418-532, fax. 419-692
Plan Holidays Treks & Expeditions
Tel. 423-599, 423-758, fax. 420-010
Royal Mount Trekking
Durbar Marg, tel. 241-452, 258-236, fax. 245-318
Sherpa Society Trekking & Society Travel
Chabahil, Chuchepati, tel. 470-361, 484-218, 472-491, fax. 470-153
Sherpa Trekking Service
Kamaladi, tel. 220-243, 227-312, fax. 227-243
Thamserku Trekking & Travel
Basundhara, Ring Road, tel. 354-491, 354-044, fax. 354-323
Topke Treks & Expeditions
Naxal, Bhagwitibahal, tel. 434-817, 434-575, fax. 434-667
Trekking Team
Thamel, tel. 227-506, fax. 228-163
Ultimate Adventures
Z Street, Thamel, tel. 438-411, 438-410
Wilderness Experience
Gyaneshwor, tel. 417-832, 416-801, fax. 417-243
Ying Yang Nature Treks & Expeditions
Tridevi Marg, Thamel, tel. 423-358, 423-359, fax. 421-701, 414-653

White-Water Rafting

Exodus Outdoor Enthusiasts
Thamel Plaza, tel. 251-753, fax. 259-244
Himalayan Whitewater
Lazimpat, tel. 426-014, 426-770, fax. 411-813
Rafting Team
Thamel, tel. 227-506, fax. 228-163
Shai River Rafting
Thamel, tel. 426-466, fax. 429-194
Ultimate Descents
Northfield Café, Thamel, tel. 419-295, fax. 411-933

NECON AIR

AIRLINES

Areoflot Russian Airlines, Kamaladi, tel. 227-399
Air France, Durbar Marg, tel. 223-339, 223-541
Air India, Hattisar, tel. 415-637
Austrian Airlines, Kamaladi, tel. 241-470, 241-506
Avia Club, tel. 412-830
Biman Bangladesh Airlines, Naxal, tel. 434-470
British Airways, Durbar Marg, tel. 226-611, 222-266
Buddha Air, Hattisar, tel. 417-802, 418-864
Cathy Pacific Airways, Kamaladi, tel. 248-944, 225-111
China Airlines, Hattisar, tel. 419-573
China Southwest Airlines, Kamaladi, tel. 419-770, 411-302
Dragonair, Durbar Marg, tel. 223-162, 223-502
Druk Air, Durbar Marg, tel. 225-166, 239-810
Emirates, Kantipath, tel. 220-579
Eva Air, Lazimat, tel. 414-318
Everest Air, Babar Mahal, tel. 226-941

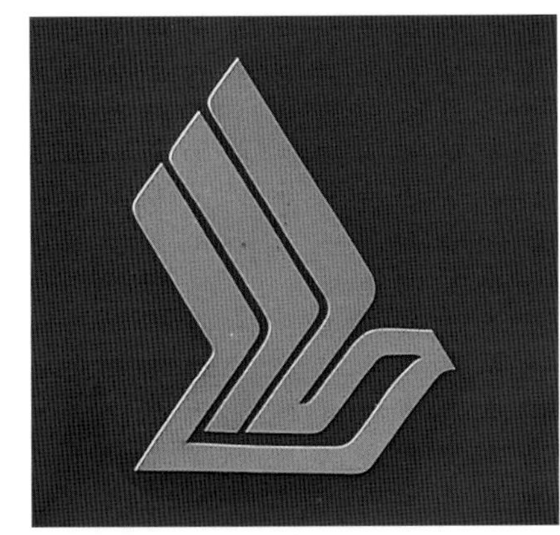

Gulf Air, Hattisar, tel. 430-456, 434-464
Indian Airlines, Hattisar, tel. 414-596, 410-906
Japan Airlines, Durbar Marg, tel. 222-838, 224-854
KLM Royal Dutch Airlines, Lekhnath Marg, tel. 418-387, 410-089
Korean Air, Kantipath, tel. 252-048, 252-049
Kuwait Airways, Kantipath, tel. 249-884
Limbini Airways, tel. 483-381, 482-728

Pakistan Internation Airlines, Durbar Marg, tel. 223-102, 227-429
Qantas Airways, Durbar Marg, tel. 220-245, 228-288
Qatar Airways, Kantipath, tel. 256-579, 257-712
Royal Brunei Airlines, Kamaladi, tel. 410-208, 413-734
Royal Nepal Airlines, Kanti Path at New Road, tel. 220-757
Saudi Arabian Airlines, Kantipath, tel. 249-387, 249-887

SAS, Kupondole, tel. 524-232, 524-732
Singapore Airlines, Durbar Marg, tel. 223-233, 220-759
Swissair, Hattisar, tel. 434-607, 434-872
Thai International Airways, Durbar Marg, tel. 223-565, 225-084, 224-387
Transavia, Kamaladi, tel. 247-215
Yeti Airways, Lazimpat, tel. 421-147, 421-215, 421-294

HELICOPTER SERVICES

Asian Airlines Helicopter, Thamal, tel. 423-273, 423-274, 416-116
Cosmic Air, Heritage Plaza, tel. 246-882, 241-051, 244-026
Dynasty Aviation, Lazimpat, tel. 410-090

Lufthansa German Airlines, Durbar Marg, tel. 223-052, 224-341
Necon Air, Sinamangal, tel. 473-860, 480-565
Nepal Airways, Naxal, tel. 412-388
Northwest Airlines, Lakhnath Marg, tel. 410-089, 418-389

Fishtail Air, Atlas Complex, Tinkune, tel. 485-186, 494-107
Gorkha Airlines, Hattisar, tel. 435-121, 435-122, 436-576, 436-579
Karnali Air Services, Sinamangal, tel, 473-141, 488-288, 491-415

EMBASSIES AND CONSULATES IN NEPAL

Australia, Bansbari, tel. 371-678, 371-466
Austria, Hattisar, tel. 434-891
Bangladesh, Maharajgunj, tel. 372-843
Belgium, Durbar Marj, tel. 228-925
Brazil, tel. 527-223
Britain, Lainchaur, tel. 411-590, 414-588

Canada, Lazimpat, tel. 415-193, 415-389
Chile, tel. 221-585
China, Baluwatar, tel. 411-740, 411-958
Cyprus, tel. 225-267, 226-327
Denmark, Baluwatar, tel. 413-010, 413-020
Egypt, Pulchowk, Lalipur, tel. 524-812, 520-083
Finland, Lazimpat, tel. 417-221, 416-636
France, Lazimpat, tel. 412-332, 418-034
Germany, Gyaneswar, tel. 416-832, 416-527
Greece, Tripureswor, tel.222-050
Hungary, Pulchowk, Lalipur, tel. 527-370, 522-871
Iceland, Ramshah Path, tel. 415-557
India, Lainchaur, tel. 410-900, 414-990

Israel, Lazimpat, tel. 411-811, 413-419
Italy, Baluwatar, tel. 412-280
Japan, Pani Pokhari, tel. 426-680
Maldives, Durbar Marg, tel. 223-045
Mexico, Pani Pokhari, tel. 412-971
Myanmar, Chakupat, Patan, tel. 524-788
Netherlands, Latitpur, tel. 522-915, 523-444
New Zealand, Dillibazar, tel. 412-436, 412-168
Norway, Jawalakhel, tel. 538-746
Pakistan, Maharajgunj, Chakrapath, tel. 374-024
Philippines, Sinamangal, tel. 478-301
Poland, Ganabahal, tel. 250-001, 250-004
Russia, Baluwatar, tel. 412-155
South Korea, Tahachal, tel. 270-172, 270-417
Spain, Battisputali, tel. 470-770
Sri Lanka, Baluwatar, tel. 413-623, 419-289
Sweden, Khichapokhari, tel. 220-939
Switzerland, Jawalakhel, tel. 524-927, 538-488
Thailand, Bansbari, tel. 371-410, 371-411
Turkey, Bijuli Bazaar, tel. 491-568, 241-964
United States, Pani Pokhari, tel. 411-179, 412-718

COMMUNICATIONS

Both sending and receiving mail is a gamble in Nepal, as letters often disappear or arrive months late. Mail to and from Europe takes around a week; ten days to the U.S. The General Post Office at Sundhara is open from 10am-5pm daily except on Saturday, closing earlier in the winter and on Fridays. Queues are often long and chaotic, and its a haven for pickpockets. You can also buy stamps at your hotel or bookstores. Outside Kathmandu mail becomes even less reliable.

The poste restante service is chaotic but functioning, American Express provides a free mail service for card and cheque-holders (PO Box 76, Kathmandu, Nepal); others must pay US$1 per enquiry. Some embassies, including the U.S., British and French, will accept letters for their citizens, or have your mail sent c/o your hotel or trekking company.

Both international telephone calls and fax services are expensive (Rs105-120 per minute for most countries) but easy. Try one of the Public Call Boxes around town offering ISD and FAX as this will be cheaper than your hotel. The Central Telegraph Office, south of the Post Office, is open 24 hours and is even cheaper. E-mail and Internet services are widely available in the main tourist areas in Kathmandu.

The local telephone service is less efficient, and what with the constant tea breaks and flexible office hours it is difficult to conduct business by]phone. Public phones located in shops charge Rs1 or Rs2 per call; others allow the use of their private phone for a slightly higher fee. There are few telephone directories. The directory assistance number is 197.

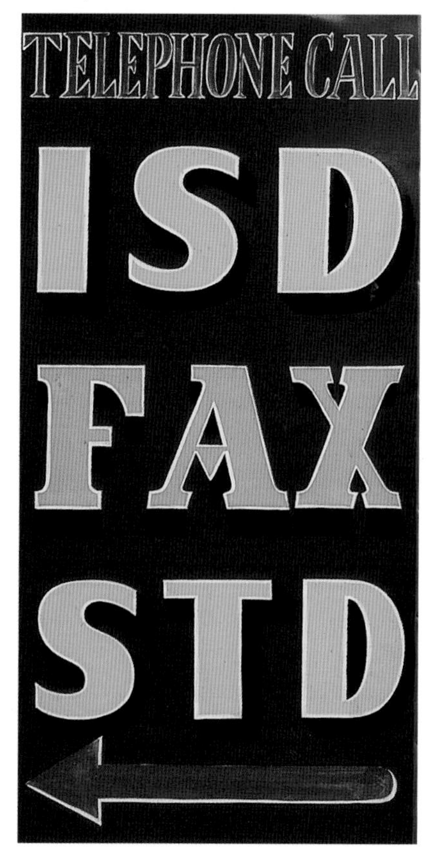

SAFETY

Until 20 years ago Nepal was virtually free of crime and violence. Though this is unfortunately changing, Nepal still remains far safer than most Western countries, especially regarding violent crime. A handful of foreigners have been attacked over the years, usually with robbery as a motive, but the odds of it happening to you are extremely low. Petty theft is a problem, however. The biggest danger is pickpockets, often deft-fingered kids who dip into your bag or pocket in the midst of a crowd. Festivals, bazaars, packed public buses, and the General Post Office are all popular locales for thieves.

Common sense is all that is necessary: be discreet with your money, and keep any valuables, including passports, airline tickets and traveller's cheques, out of sight and in a safe place (larger hotels have safes). Minimize the amount of money you carry with you, or carry it in a money-belt next to your body (inside your clothing) and have change available for minor purchases or taxis to avoid showing the entire bank.

Women travellers can feel quite safe, though verbal harassment and the occasional grope is increasing in Kathmandu.

Nepali and Tibetan Terms

avatar incarnation or manifestation of a deity
bahal Newari Buddhist monastery complex
baksheesh a tip; often a tip given in advance to expedite service-more bluntly, a bribe
bhajan religious hymn
Bhotia, Bhotiya, Bhotey, general term for Tibetan-influenced people of the northern border regions
bodhisattva a buddha-to-be who has renounced individual enlightenment to help other beings
chaitya a Buddhist monument, a miniature version of a stupa
chang (Tib.) home-made beer, usually brewed from barley
chautara shady trailside resting place with a low wall to support porters' loads
chorten (Tib.) a small stupa, sometimes with a passage through the middle so that people can walk through it
chowk a square or courtyard
dal bhat The national dish of Nepal: lentils (dal) and cooked rice (bhat), served with curried vegetables
dhara water tap
doko wicker basket used for carrying loads
dorje (Tib.) see vajra
dyochem (Newari) 'god's house', a special shrine
gainey a minstrel caste
ghat flight of stone steps lining river banks, used for laundry, bathing and cremation
gompa (Tib.) Tibetan Buddhist monastery
guthi traditional Newari social association
hiti sunken fountain typical of the Kathmandu Valley
jatra festival
khukri Curved Nepali knife
kora (Tib.) circumambulation
Kumari young virgin Buddhist girl worshipped as a manifestation of the Hindu goddess Durga
ladoo a milk-based sweet
lama (Tib.) guru; religious teacher
Licchavi a *ruling dynasty of the Kathmandu Valey (AD 300-879)*
linga symbol related to Shiva and the phallus
makara sea serpents of Hindu mythology
mandala mystic diagram depicting the order of the universe
mani wall prayer wall: heap of flat stones engraved with mantra and religious images, found in mountainous Buddhist regions
mantra mystic formula of Sanskrit syllables
math Hindu monastery
mela fair, often associated with a religious festival
momo (Tib.) meat-stuffed dumplings
naga serpent deities: guardians of wealth associated with rain
pati open resthouse providing shelter to travellers
puja ritual offering and prayer
rakshi (Tib. arak) potent alcoholic drink distilled from grain
sal hardwood tree famed for its fine-grained wood
samsara the cycle of delusion created by the unenlightened mind
sadhu Hindu ascetic or holy man
shikhara a tapered tower surmounting a temple
shikar the hunt
sindhur red powder used as religious offering
sirdar organizer of a trek or expedition
stupa Buddhist monument: a hemispheric mound topped by a conical spire
tantra school of mysticism developed in medieval India which has influenced both Hinduism and Buddhism
tempo three-wheeled motor vehicle serving as an public taxi
thangka (Tib.) scroll painting depicting religious subjects
tika auspicious mark on the forehead, made as part of worship
tol neighbourhood or quarter of a city
tongba drink made from hot water mixed with fermented mash
torana semicircular carved tympanum mounted over temple doors and windows
topi Nepali men's cap, brimless and slightly lopsided
tsampa (Tib.) roasted barley flour, a highland staple
yaksha graceful nymph of Hindu mythology
vajra Buddhist ritual implement representing the absolute aspect of reality

Hindu and Buddhist Deities

Ajima Newari grandmother goddesses; indigenous deities often placated with blood sacrifice

Annapurna goddess of the harvest, a manifestation of **Lakshmi**

Ashta Matrika 'Eight Mothers', each representing a different aspect of Durga

Avalokitesvara compassionate Bodhisattva who grew eleven heads and 1,000 arms in order to help suffering beings; see **Lokesvara**

Bhagwati another name for the goddess **Durga**

Bhairab fierce manifestation of **Shiva**

Bhimsen patron god of traders: a minor figure in the Mahabharata

Buddha an enlightened being; more particularly the historical Buddha, Siddhartha Gautama

Bunga Dyo local name for **Machhendranath**

Chandeswari fierce goddess associated with Durga, slayer of the demon Chand

Devi another name for the goddess **Durga** or **Parvati**

Durga The Great Goddess, appearing in many different manifestations, most popularly as the defeater of the evil buffalo demon Mahisasura.

Ganesh elephant-headed god of luck, son of **Shiva** and **Parvati**

Ganga goddess associated with the sacred River Ganges, usually appearing with Jamuna, the personification of another sacred Indian river

Garuda winged man, the mount of **Vishnu**

Goraknath 12th-century yogi deified as an aspect of **Shiva**

Guru Rinpoche *see* **Padmasambhava**

Guyheswari the Secret Goddess, a name for **Shiva's** spouse Sati

Hanuman the Monkey King, a prominent figure in the Ramayana, worshipped as a protector

Indra Vedic deity honoured as King of the Gods

Kali the 'Black One', hideous goddess personifying death

Krishna blue-complexioned god of love, an incarnation of **Vishnu**

Kumari young virgin worshipped as an incarnation of **Durga**

Lakshmi goddess of wealth and abundance, consort of **Vishnu**

Lokesvara (Lokeswar, Karunamaya) 'Lord of the World', beloved bodhisattva and god of compassion

Machhendranath rainmaking patron deity of the Kathmandu Valley, worshipped primarily by Buddhist Newars

Mai indigenous deities transformed into 'Mother Goddesses', usually associated with a particular locality

Manjushri bodhisattva and embodiment of wisdom and learning

Nandi mount of Shiva, depicted as a kneeling bull

Narasimha incarnation of Vishnu, half man, half lion

Padmapani lotus-holding bodhisattva; see **Lokesvara**

Padmasambhava Indian tantric responsible for the introduction of Buddhism into Tibet

Pancha Buddha five Buddhas, each associated with a different element, colour, direction and aspect of enlightenment

Parvati consort of **Shiva** and a goddess in her own right

Pashupati (nath) Lord of the Beasts, benevolent form of **Shiva**

Saraswati goddess of learning and culture

Shiva important Hindu deity, the transformer and destroyer

Sitala goddess of smallpox and protector of children; Newari Buddhists worship her as Harati

Taleju tantric goddess imported from India and made patron of the Malla dynasty; related to **Durga**

Tara (Tib. **Dolma**) female bodhisattva representing mercy and compassion, appearing in 21 emanations, the most important being the White and Green Taras

Vajra Yogini Tantric Buddhist deity, a fierce protector goddess

Vishnu an important Hindu god worshipped as the Preserver and appearing in 10 principal incarnations